Empowered Parents Empowering Kids

A Guide to **Be You** Parenting

by Mary Dravis-Parrish

ACCESS
CONSCIOUSNESS®
PUBLISHING

Empowered Parents Empowering Kids
Copyright © 2015 Mary Dravis-Parrish
ISBN: 978-1-63493-013-0

Published by
Access Consciousness Publishing, LLC
www.accessconsciousnesspublishing.com

Printed in the United States of America

Advance acclaim for

Empowered Parents Empowering Kids

I believe Empowered Parents Empowering Kids *is for everyone who interacts with, or has ever had children. I guess that means everyone! I have gained a new perspective on how to be myself while parenting and interacting with children. All of the tools such as asking questions have become a way of life and the resulting positive shifts have been life changing.*

~ Nancy Evans, RN, BSN, CH — Founder Open Pathways to Learning

I greatly appreciated the gentleness of Mary's words, suggestions and the allowance I have received to BE the parent that works for me, my children and my family. What great tools these are to be able to use and teach my children how they can be independent, aware and make choices that will work and benefit them. Plus I get that benefit too! I am so thankful Mary has written Empowered Parents Empowering Kids. *I now know more how to be the parent I always wanted to be, but had let others' beliefs, opinions and my guilt get in the way. If you're a parent who feels like you have tried everything in regards to parenting, then you have not read this book yet. A must read with incredible tools that actually work and create more ease in parenting!*

~ Alyssa McCall, LMT — Mother of two active boys

I have read a lot of parenting books and they have all been pretty much the same. Empowered Parents Empowering Kids *is very different. It gives very specific, detailed information without being overwhelming. It is not focused on any particular age group, the tools work well for all ages. I recommend it not just for parents but for anyone who works with or spends time with children.*

~ Jodi N. — Parent, grandparent

Empowered Parents, Empowering Kids *showed me it is possible to have me, parent children, plus other things in my life, with joy and well-being — even if I don't know exactly what or how. Your writing has helped change my perspective by applying Access Consciousness® tools to family situations in an organized sort of way. You have succeeded in convincing me that "special needs" labels do not mean the tools cannot be useful, that it is about creative process and not hard and fast rules. I will be rereading* Empowered Parents Empowering Kids *to remind myself of its many useful tips. What else is possible?*

~ G. D. Khalsa — Mother of special needs child

"Today you are you!

That is truer than true!

There is no one alive

who is you-er than you!

~ Dr. Seuss

In Gratitude

This book wouldn't have been possible without my personal experiences raising my three sons, Jason, Ben and Robb; who chose me to be their mother. I am also grateful to my husband Steve, for allowing me to be a part of his parenting life with his children Anna and Eric. And what would my parenting experience be if not for the parents I chose? Many thanks for all that I learned from my parents: Bob and Carol. Thank you for all that you have contributed to my life adventure of self-discovery through family living.

To Gary Douglas, founder of Access Consciousness®, I express deep gratitude for his dedication to bringing more consciousness to our planet. Using the tools of Access Consciousness® offers a new possibility for family living that can change the world. I extend heartfelt thanks to Dr. Dain Heer for his contribution to Access and his own insights from his book: *Being You, Changing the World*®. It has added to my inspiration in directing this message to parents and kids.

Thank you to my reviewers who so diligently gave me feedback about the contents. Thank you, Alyssa, Holly, Jodi, Cheryl, Dhan and Nancy. I also acknowledge a huge thank-you to my brother,

Ted Brockish, and Simone Anna Padur, who graciously assisted me with the editing of these pages.

Most importantly I'd like to thank the parents who have entrusted to me their lives, their stories, their struggles and their triumphs in order to emerge empowered and thus empowering their children to create a better world. Your courage and efforts have been noticed and are sending ripple effects throughout the world. For this I thank you and I wish you all abundant joy in your adventure in living.

Contents

~1~

BE YOU *Parenting*

The adventure unfolds...

Congratulations you are a parent! Whether you are a new parent, a parent of teens or adults, you have been chosen. As an act of free will, your children chose you to be their parent. They did not come with a manual, which can cause confusion for parents as they discover that each child requires something different. In addition, some kids are not receptive to the same way their parents were parented. In this frustration and confusion many parents turn to experts to tell them how to raise their children. Although many "experts" may have good advice, what if you already know all you need to know in order to be the best parent for your child?

Be You Parenting: means being in allowance of you and acting according to what is true for you, not the world outside of you. When you parent from that place you empower your children to be who they truly **be**. I am writing this book not to tell you how to parent but rather how to discover more of you so that you can parent without losing you in the equation. I can't think of a better win-win for families.

Many of us avoid looking at ourselves in the mirror because we don't like what we see, and if we don't see it, we don't have to do anything to change it. What if by looking in the mirror you were able to see the parts of you that aren't really you? What if you can begin to change so that YOU can show up? What you do with the image you see is up to you. I have found it to be more to my benefit, and thus to my children's benefit, to look deeper and see what it is I don't like about the image I see and begin to change it. A wise teacher told me that whether you are a parent, teacher, counselor or good friend, you are at your best for others when you are focusing and being the best you that **you** can be. That has been my experience. It doesn't mean that you stay the same, but rather that you are always on a quest to be more of you. You continue to explore and learn more about what would improve your life and how you could choose to live it.

Have you ever thought you had to know it all in order to be any good at anything? I certainly did. Even as I thought about writing this book, I wondered if I knew "enough" to share my insights with other parents. Even though that sounds pretty silly as I share those words, I have found others who share the same underlying belief. What if you already know all you need to know for this moment and the rest will come as you seek and ask? Once this is acknowledged life becomes much easier. I discovered that I do not need to constantly judge myself in order to change. I create new possibilities and choices by asking questions. Don't worry if you are wondering how that is done. I would like to acknowledge that you are doing the best you know how to do with the knowledge and experience you have so far. How much more are you capable of being if you are open and willing to do and be even more? We will go through this step by step together.

This book comes out of spending a lifetime of over 40 years not only parenting my own children, but also sharing that journey with numerous parents. I have laughed and cried with parents as we frantically searched for the correct path of "perfect parenting." We were looking outside of ourselves for someone to tell us how to parent so that our kids would turn out "perfectly." That word "perfect" carries such judgment and condemnation. When in fact, each moment is "perfect" in and of itself, just as we are — in whatever place we find ourselves. Our moments and experiences need not be judged whether they are perfect or not. Can you be all right with that? If you can't, that may be the place you can begin to apply some of these tools.

This book is dedicated to YOU! What if you are the parent your kids require, just by being you? What if your kids are what you require now in order to know more of who you truly be? I have a sense that you will come to know that you do know how to BE the parent you and your kids would like you to BE. You have been the master creator in your life through the choices that you have made. As the master creator, you also get to shift, change, transform and be empowered as the infinite being you are. How is that for adventure?

It is my desire that this book gives you a direction to create the change you desire. I will share with you techniques, tools and ideas as a springboard from which you can dive in and begin to play and expand to make it all your own. In addition, these tips will also guide you to empower your children to grow, discover and choose the life they would like to have. How cool is that? Have fun along the way — it is allowed — and keep in mind your kids know more than you think they do! This is about creating your own parenting method, the one that works for you. You might be surprised with what you discover. It just might make life more fun and bring more joy and ease as well. Would you be willing to have more fun, joy and ease show up in your life?

Before digging in, I want to further acknowledge my sources for this book. I have read many books, listened to many experts, and have tried many methods. I was fortunate to meet Gary Douglas and Dr. Dain Heer, the founders of Access Consciousness®, in 2010. Access offers tools and processes with a focus on being more conscious and being more of who we truly be. I have found applying these tools to the role of parenting allows for more **Be You Parenting** in a way that I have not found in any other parent resources. As I began to implement the tools and processes of Access Consciousness® in my life and the lives of my clients, I began to see incredible changes. People began to let go of their judgments with ease. They were less stressed and a real joy was taking over. For myself, since I began using these tools, I have never been happier, healthier, and more empowered to live my life for me. I am discovering how to BE ME! It only made sense that utilizing tools that allow you to choose what works best for you in this life can make family life easier and happier. The challenge comes with acknowledging that you can have all of you and parent at the same time. Not everyone is willing to be that, but for those who are, get ready for the adventure of your life!

~2~

Parenting Is an Adventure

"Here's to freedom, cheers to art. Here's to having an excellent adventure and may the stopping never start."
— Jason Mraz

Are you ready to have the adventure of a lifetime? Being a parent is certainly a different adventure than people who don't have children. Children give us the opportunity to see ourselves as no one else can. Kids by nature are experts at mimicking all of the faults, judgments and beliefs we carry in life. Depending on how we approach the role of parenting, these precious little beings give us the opportunity to step into a world of possibilities.

There are many different "styles" of parenting. In my search to be the best parent I could be, I came across terms in parenting programs that applied to different ways of parenting such as: the "helicopter" parent, the authoritarian parent, the permissive parent and the uninvolved parent. Perhaps you have heard of these descriptions too. Each of these styles, although having different qualities, have similar results — children are not happy and are definitely not empowered or encouraged to live a life that is of their creation. Not only that, the parents are not happy and are not living a life they enjoy! These parents are motivated by something other than being them. They do not seem to understand that parenting is an adventure and worthy of exploration, not exploitation.

If you find yourself as one of these styles, no worries, I am not here to judge you, but rather to ask some important questions. Is it working? Are you and your children happy? If what you are doing as a parent is working for you, the only thing I would suggest is occasionally check in with your kids to see if what you are doing is working for them too. Are your kids living their lives based on your expectations and desires? All too often our offspring want to make us happy so they put on a mask of being happy. However, there are usually clues along the way to let a parent know that something is amiss. Also check in with your happiness. Is your happiness dependent on anyone else — your spouse, your partner, your kids, your friends, or your family? Or can you choose to be happy at any moment?

Being a parent is an adventure that is different from people who don't have children. Parents get the opportunity to be enriched with the presence of unique beings entering their family experience. The target for parents is to nurture each person in your family with trust, allowance, honor and gratitude.

How do you experience the differences that each relationship brings to the world and still honor each other? You may have started this adventure when you took on a partner in life and through that relationship you may have discovered that adding another person to your daily life can be rewarding. It also brings with it the challenge of being in allowance of each other and resisting the urge to change that other person. Our adventure with our children is the similar. They may not be aware yet of their journey or purpose in this lifetime. These kids will look to you to guide them as they discover what that is for them. Some children come to their parents and know and are aware of themselves and their gifts. These kids will look to you to support and encourage them. I found that each of my three sons were very different. I want to reassure you that being you will make this adventure much easier and much more fun than it may appear on the outside. Even though each person in your family is different, what they truly require from you is the same — you being you. So let's get on with exploring and uncovering the parent that is truly you!

The big question is whether you are going to be able to say
a hearty yes to your adventure.
— Joseph Campbell

In this book there are places for you to write down ideas, practices, and questions. You may choose to use a separate journal so you can come back to these sections again. As you move into your own awareness, your perspective changes and you get to witness how you change.

 You will see this picture when I introduce a tool that you can put into your knapsack to carry with you through life. Since you may not be used to using these tools, it is only fair that you give yourself time to practice and play with each tool. **Try not to judge it or yourself but just play with it.** Be like a child — curious and inquisitive ... which brings us to the first tool.

~3~

The Importance of Question

"A question empowers, an answer disempowers."
— Gary Douglas, Founder of Access
Consciousness®

Asking questions is a powerful way to empower oneself. When you ask a question you tell the Universe that you are willing to receive infinite possibilities to change a situation, to gain awareness, or to have more insight. I will start by giving you some questions. As you ask the questions, refrain from answering; rather allow awareness and possibility to come to you. Don't worry about having the "right answer" as these questions do not have "right or wrong answers," just awareness of possibilities from which you can choose what is true for you. This is a place to play and not a place to judge you. The more willing you are to allow whatever shows up; the more benefit you will receive.

Ready? Let's begin:

What reason did you choose to become a parent?

Maybe you consciously planned to become a parent or maybe, like me, it didn't seem like a choice but something that happened to you. I became pregnant at the age of 17, and I really didn't think that I had purposely chosen to become a teen parent. Many years later I asked myself, "What reason did I choose to become a parent at age 17?" I did have reasons. One reason that became evident was that it was my way of avoiding going to college. In my eyes, it was the expectation for every child in our family to go to college. I didn't know what I wanted to do with my life at that point and I didn't have enough confidence to believe in myself. I didn't want to fail. So I created a way out. I had watched and helped my mother care for my siblings, and I believed that I could probably be successful being a mom. And there I was 17 and pregnant. Was I cognitive of these thoughts or beliefs? No, but it was how I aligned with my beliefs at the time. I have become aware through the years that there are more reasons for my choices, but this gives you an idea of how we can create our reality with our beliefs or points of view.

Some parents were brought up as kids with the expectation that it is "normal" to get married and to have kids. And how many people then went out to find their mate and begin to live a "normal life"? It isn't acceptable to be different and abnormal. People would judge and wonder what was wrong if you didn't go out and get married and have kids. And this would be the reason that they became parents. Is there a belief that to be normal, a person gets married and has kids? And does the work for everyone?

As you become aware of your reasons, you may discover aspects and beliefs in your life that you would like to change. You then have the choice to change or not. If you aren't coming up with your reasons, stay with it and at some point you will get awareness. Just be aware of any information that may come to you.

Ask: "Truth, what reason did I choose to become a parent?"

 I include the word "truth" when asking questions because we can try to lie to ourselves in order to avoid what is really true. When we ask "truth," we are inviting the truth to come forth.

Write your reflections.

_____

_____

_____

_____

_____

_____

_____

_____

_____

_____

_____

_____

_____

_____

_____

_____

_____

_____

_____

_____

_____

_____

_____

_____

_____

_____

Once you have asked this question and you are willing to receive the awareness and insight it brings up, you can then get in touch with what is true for you. Look at what comes through for you, and as you sit with it. Does it bring a sense of "Ah," expansive-open space with it? Does it feel true for you even if it doesn't seem to make sense? Keep in mind that this isn't about analyzing why something comes up; it's about checking in and seeing what is true for you.

Keep asking more questions to go deeper if you like. Questions like: **"Do I need to know anything else about this?"** or **"What else do I need to know that will help me discover more about my choice to be a parent?"** You are asking only for information that will contribute to your awareness of change, not to understand it all. Many of us analyze things endlessly, only to add more judgment of ourselves by having good or bad reasons for what we chose. That is not the purpose of asking. In these questions we are asking to have the awareness to acknowledge that we did indeed have a choice in becoming parents, and choice is not something to be judged.

Here is another example. A father of two was doing this reflection exercise and the awareness came to him that he chose to be a parent because it was what was expected in order to have a happy life. When he came face to face with this awareness, he knew it was why he chose to be a parent. He didn't realize at the time that he could choose something else. Perhaps you have seen or heard expectations like "When are you going to get married and have a family?" He recognized that he bought all of that as the way he should live his life, and once he became a father, he realized that it wasn't really what he wanted for his life. This was an insightful awareness for him that allowed him to make other choices about his life and how he wanted to parent his children.

Now let's explore some other questions about being parents. Simply follow the same format as above with these questions or any other questions that arise in this process.

Truth ...

- **What expectations do I have about being a parent?**

- **Do I parent just like my parents?**

- **Do I resist parenting like my parents?**

- **What do I want/expect from my kids?**

_____

_____

_____

_____

_____

_____

_____

_____

_____

_____

_____

_____

_____

Are you getting some good insights? Remember that you are just gathering information. There is no need to judge any of this. As you move through these questions you can star or check any awareness that you want to spend more time with later.

Now continue with these questions:

Truth ...

- **Do I need my kids to fulfill my expectation of myself?**

- **Do I expect my kids to make my life perfect?**

- **Do my kids need me in order to have a fulfilling life?**

- **Do I want to have fun parenting or do I see it as a serious role?**

_____

_____

_____

_____

_____

_____

_____

_____

_____

_____

_____

_____

_____

_____

_____

_____

_____

_____

_____

_____

At one of my workshops, we asked these questions and it became clear for one parent that she had created a "need" in having and raising her children. She had created the idea that her kids needed her so much that she ended up smothering her kids with control and distrust, and building a life that only consisted of her kids. As a result she felt disconnected from her spouse; and her children were always whining at her about one thing or another. She complained that she was constantly tired of having to make sure they all did what they needed to do to be "successful."

Once she gained the insight about the need she had created, this woman could begin to step into a willingness to let that go and choose to parent from a different perspective. This new perspective involved getting to know more of who she is and not defining herself as just being a mother. She started to discover other talents and interests that she has. As she started to choose to include herself in her life, her children began to calm down and become less dependent on her and they felt more empowered to be themselves. The woman found she had renewed energy to devote to herself and her adult relationships. She could see the gift of receiving other people from a place of being rather than out of need. This greatly impacted her life in a very beneficial way.

As you ask these questions, don't be surprised if other questions come up. In this process, you get a better idea of how you are being a parent. It all has a value to you or you wouldn't choose it. Here are some insights you will want to pay attention to:

- **Am I defending who I am? (good parent vs. bad parent).**

- **Am I proving that I can parent differently from my parents?**

- **Am I defending my parents as perfect parents because I have turned out all right? If so, am I parenting like they did even though it may not work for me, or my family?**

- **Am I judging any of my choices by defending or proving them for any reason?**

Pay attention to those insights that raise some emotion, feel uncomfortable or put you in the position of "Yeah, but…" as a way of defending your choices. When you are defending, realize that you may have judgments about that choice and the target is to let go of those judgments so you can be more for you and your family. While you are doing these questions notice how it feels to let go of judgments. What is different? Watch out, though, it may create more space and fun in your life.

And the last questions we will address in this area are:

Truth…

- **What is my point of view about how I currently parent?**

- **What is my confidence level with parenting?**

- **What do I wish I could do differently but I just don't seem to know how?**

I encourage you to spend as much time as you need on the above questions as a beginning point for the rest of this book. Feel free to take time to allow the awareness to come, and remember you can come back to this at any time. Awareness usually shows up when you're not focused on getting an answer. For me, awareness and insights come while I am waking up in the morning, or in the shower, or driving. Do things that will get your thinking mind out of the way so you can receive the information you truly seek.

I understand you may feel an urgent need to "fix" a certain situation in your family. And while you may be concerned about your child's behavior, going through this process will allow you to get to the place where you can effectively perceive and know how to handle that situation. If you have a relationship that is out of sorts, taking the time now will shed light on what is really happening as you begin to see what you are adding to the equation in the form of your beliefs and points of view.

My experience is that it is most beneficial to begin with the beliefs you hold currently. When I began this process, I was wondering about many of the beliefs that I had grown up with and had just automatically assumed they would work for me too. I questioned my religious faith as well as the norms that society tells us are required to have a happy, successful life. All of these beliefs had a part in form-ing who I was in that moment. They were the points of view that I owned in order to create the reality that I was living.

Acknowledge and even embrace your beliefs and points of view for what they are and where they have brought you to this point in life. What if you recognize that you are the creator of your life? And what if the choices you have up to this point have made your life extraor-dinary? With some added awareness and additional tools, you will be able to expand your creativity to new levels that serve you and your family. As you release and let go of the limiting beliefs that you have been holding in place, your life may look different from what you originally planned. It may be much more phenomenal than you ever thought possible.

Asking questions will give you the insight you need to create the changes you desire. You could even make note of the things that are showing up that you would like to change. Perhaps you would like to be more patient, more caring, gentler, more confident, and more aware. As you create your list, you may become aware of other changes that you would like to make. Gary Douglas suggests people use these four questions to gain more awareness and clarity for whatever is going on. Simply ask,

1. **"What is this?"**

 2. **"What do I do with this?"**

3. **"Can I change this?"**

4. **"If so how do I change this?"**

These four questions have been a constant in my life. I ask them for all kinds of things from being frustrated with my computer to knowing how to assist my child through a difficult time. These questions will become your friends as you go through this book and your journey through life. Just by asking these questions and being open to receive from them will allow new possibilities and awareness to show up that may surprise you. If you find yourself wanting to figure out the answers to your questions, be aware — that is where you stop the energy of change the question can be. You are trying to force something to happen that you have decided should happen. This will cut you off from other possibilities that could be more to your benefit, which may not be in your best interest.

Many people aren't raised to ask questions in this manner. The closest I came to asking questions in this manner was through prayer. And that was different because I was usually asking for what I wanted to have happen rather than being willing to allow possibilities to come forth and then choosing from those possibilities. So don't be surprised if your question muscle is weak. It is like anything new, it takes practice. Knowing you want to be the best parent you can **BE** will be the reminder to do your question exercises to strengthen that muscle. As you practice using questions, you will begin to use them with your children and begin to ask them to ask questions so that they can receive from the infinite possibilities. Now there's a gift worth exercising for!

As we continue on this journey, keep the notes you take available as it will allow you to apply future tools, techniques and processes that are included in this book. Now that you have begun the process of identifying areas of beliefs that you may be ready to let go of, I see no reason to have you hold onto them any longer. I will share with you in the next chapter a process I use from Access Consciousness®. It has worked magically for me and many others that I have worked with one on one as well as in workshops and classes.

~4~

You Are the Creator of Your Life

**"You are essentially who you create yourself
to be, and all that occurs in your life is
the result of your own making."**
— Stephen Richards

 Being the creator of your own life brings meaning to the tool I am about to introduce to you. It is the concept that if I am the creator of my life, then I also get to destroy and uncreate anything that is no longer working.

I am very thankful I learned how to destroy and uncreate from Gary Douglas. At first, the term "destroy and uncreate" seemed harsh and violent to me until I explored it further. First, I had to acknowledge that I am the creator of my life. I was creating my life based on my beliefs and judgments or what Access Consciousness® calls points of view. Everyone has them, and we all use them to create each of our realities. If you consider that your points of view create your reality then if you want to create something different you have to change your point of view. Sometimes that is easy to do, and sometimes assistance is appreciated. As the creator of your life, you have the choice to destroy and uncreate anything that doesn't work in your life and to create the masterpiece that does work for you. You are like an artist who can choose to destroy a piece of pottery or piece of music, or a painting that doesn't match the vision. You can choose to re-create a version that matches the masterpiece desired. You can repeat it as often as you like since you are constantly changing and creating. You are the Master Creator of your life.

Recently, I worked with a mother, who, when using these tools, began to see how she was creating the chaos in her life by choosing to be overprotective toward her children. She had created a "need" that kept her and her children chained to each other. When I asked her if she was ready to destroy and uncreate the need she had created, she said, "Yes!" There needs to be a desire and a willingness to destroy and uncreate for something else can be created. When you can begin to see that some of your creations aren't working for you or your family, you can take this step to begin the process of changing it.

It is in the choice of being willing to say, "Yes," which allows the energy shifts and new possibilities to occur. This mother went on from there to ask questions about the origin of this "need" she had created. Her childhood had been one that left her empty and feeling as if she didn't have a purpose. She created a need that would allow her to fill that emptiness. Her life was dependent on having others need her. The emptiness didn't really fill up, she just didn't know how else to be more of her. Through the question process, she began to see that this "need" was actually keeping her from creating a life that allowed her to be all of her. By destroying and uncreating that "need" she and her children could be set free from the chaos she had created. She continues to use the tools so that now she can be and do the things that fill her with joy and pleasure.

Please note that your children are not your creation. Therefore, you cannot choose to destroy and uncreate them. If you are treating your children as if they are your creation then you are limiting their capacity to create their own life. Imagine being on the receiving end of that! It is not surprising that many adults grew up **not** knowing that they were and are the creators of their own lives. They have also missed out on the awareness of all they have created; and all they are capable of creating. What if that could be different for you and your children? What if you acknowledge your children as the creators of their own lives? What if you could show them that they too can destroy and uncreate what doesn't work for them?

How do you use this tool? By simply acknowledging what isn't working for you. Remember the questions you asked as we started this process? Did you have an awareness come up? This is a good place for you to start. Here is an example: a parent discovers they are parenting from proving they can parent better than they were parented. By becoming aware of this they can then choose to change it.

 To use this tool, simply say,

"Everything this belief brings up about how I parent, am I willing to destroy and uncreate it?" Answer "yes." Now for the added punch to truly change this you can use The Clearing Statement® from Access Consciousness® that works like a giant eraser and takes the point of creation, the point of destruction along with all the judgments and erases them away. To use the clearing statement just add **Right and Wrong, Good and Bad, POD and POC, All 9, Shorts, Boys and Beyonds.®**

Say what? What were those words and what do they mean? I will give you a brief explanation here and then you can find a more detailed explanation at www.theclearingstatement.com.

This clearing statement addresses all the places where you have used judgment — right or wrong, good or bad — to form a fixed point of view or a belief. There are 9 layers (all 9's) of points of view you have taken to justify this belief. Then there is the Point of Creation (POC) where you actually bought the belief as real and created it. The Point of Destruction (POD) is the place where this belief began to destroy your life and stopped working for you. Have you ever made something so meaningful or meaningless that you pushed away your awareness of what was really true? That is the Shorts part of the statement. The Beyonds includes those times you have gone to a place where it all just seemed so beyond your understanding that you allowed it to control you. So, when you ask a question or think about something that is limiting you or not working for you, there is an energy that comes up. You can think of it as hitting the delete button on a computer and clearing away the out-dated files that no longer work for you. The energy comes up, you run the clearing statement, and then you have a whole lot more space from which to create anything you choose!

Here is another clearing around proving:

All the places that I have been proving myself right by proving my parents to be wrong, will I destroy and uncreate all of that?

Right and Wrong, Good and Bad, POD and POC, All 9, Shorts, Boys and Beyonds.®

And for those who have created "need' in their life:

Everywhere I have created my children as the source of my need in order to be me will I destroy and uncreate all of that?

Right and Wrong, Good and Bad, POD and POC, All 9, Shorts, Boys and Beyonds.®

When you limit yourself, you feel contracted and small. As you do this process, you may begin to sense that the limitations around that point of view will subside and create more expansive space from which you get to choose something different. It may take several repetitions of the statement since you hold these beliefs on various levels and apply them to different aspects of your life. But with repetition, many people find they release and discover they are no longer affected by the belief and are free to create something new or respond in a different way.

As you read these clearings, there may be certain ones that you sense more energy on than others. If that happens, it means those clearings have more capacity for change in your life. It can be beneficial to repeat any or all of those clearings over and over to create the change you are looking for. I have found some clearings especially assist me in changing if I run them 30 times for 30 days. This is easier to accomplish when I record them and create a loop that I can listen to while I work or sleep. You can find apps for smart phones that will do this, or you can create your own playlist.

This may be an opportune time to go back over the questions and look at the ones that you notice carry some sticky energy or bring up some emotions. You can apply "destroy and uncreate" and use the clearing statement for all of them. Once you start doing this, pay attention in the minutes, hours, days and weeks that follow. Are things different in these areas and or other areas of your life? You will be able to apply this tool as we continue to explore other aspects of your life that may not be working for you. So put the clearing statement in your knapsack along with your questions as we go onward in this adventure of parenting and discovery.

What creations are you willing to destroy and uncreate? What would you like to create instead?

_____

_____

_____

_____

~5~

Stop Pushing My Buttons

"If parents have problems with their child's behavior and all they have in their parental tool kit are bigger hammers, the kids are going to develop bigger nails."
— James Lehman, MSW

Do your kids push your buttons, drain your energy, and leave you wondering what just happened? Just who is in control? Parenting children need not be so confusing or frustrating.

Think about a time when you felt controlled, confused, and maybe even angry that your child took control of you. As you recall one of those times, notice the sensations you feel in your body. Just notice what is there. Is there a place in your body that you feel it the most?

Everyone is different, so don't feel that you need to have the "right" answer and if you don't feel anything that's all right too. You don't need to do anything with that right now, just be aware of it. I'll come back to it later. As well as being you, it is important to connect with your physical body; this is how you get in touch with your knowing. It allows you to get out of your head and stop trying to think things through.

Take a moment and write down a situation that comes to mind where you found yourself losing control with your kids or feeling helpless, frustrated, confused or anxious. Make a note of the sensations that come up as you recall the event.

_____

_____

_____

_____

_____

_____

_____

_____

_____

_____

_____

_____

_____

_____

_____

_____

_____

_____

_____

_____

_____

_____

Asking questions creates a shift in the energy. A question will change the energy from the limitations you are creating with confusion, worry and frustration and allow a different possibility to show up. You will find that possibilities you wouldn't have thought of on your own will begin to come forth. The key to asking questions is to allow the possibilities to show up without trying to figure it all out. This is the part that becomes easy. You can now stop analyzing, comparing and forcing a decision.

Phew!

That's a load off! Many people do way too much thinking instead of allowing and letting the natural flow to happen. A Universal Truth is Ask and you shall receive, however, many people will ask and then go into figuring out the answer. That is when they analyze, compare and judge until they often talk themselves out of possibilities and miss receiving the gift of the possibilities, from which they could choose. Sound familiar?

Everywhere I have been over thinking everything instead of using my knowing and choosing, will I destroy and uncreate all of that?

Right and Wrong, Good and Bad, POD and POC, All 9, Shorts, Boys and Beyonds.®

Asking works better if you ask and then wait, pay attention and be willing to receive. Be aware that when you ask for something, in order for it to show up, you do need to be willing to have it or it won't really come to you. We will talk more about receiving in chapter 12.

What kinds of questions do you ask? This does matter. In order to receive, you aren't going to be using any "why" questions but rather questions that open you up to possibility and change. When asking "why," you are really going back and trying to figure it all out, thinking that if you can understand it, you can change it. **So ask yourself: Truth, will my understanding this change this?** Check in. Have you been programed that understanding something will create the solution? How has that been working for you? What is your awareness here? How many things do you have going on in your life that you don't understand and yet they seem to work just as they need to?

Gary reminded me that there is so much that we try to figure out in our heads. Let's face it if we could have used our minds to change things by figuring them out, wouldn't we have done it already? If you are reading this book, you have probably tried that by now and discovered that it doesn't really work. You can't store in your mind all that the Universe knows and works from. You can, however, access that through your asking. Have you ever known something without knowing in your head how you knew it? What if you know more than you think you know?

Another reason not to use the question "why" is that we lose sight of the truth. Have you ever asked your child why she did something? Right away she needs to go into defending what she did or figure out a way to make her choice and her look good. What if we do the same thing when we ask ourselves why we chose something? Will we be truthful or will we avoid what we know because we don't want to judge ourselves? What if we didn't ask "why"? You will see the format I suggest for the questions as a model for forming your questions.

Now let's go back to the situation you wrote down. What kind of questions could you use that would shift you to a place where you can empower you and your child? I have listed some below that you can use to get started or you may magically come up with your own.

Let's practice. Review your situation and connect with the sensation in your body; now choose a question to ask. Notice what happens to the sensation. Does it lighten up? Or does it go away completely or nothing at all? Just notice; it is all part of the practice.

Questions to change anything:

- What is this?

- What do I do with this?

- Can I change this? If so how?

- What else is possible?®

- What is right about (my family, my child, me, this situation) that I am not willing to acknowledge?

- What can I receive from this (person, situation,) that I haven't been willing to receive?

- What is right about this I'm not getting?

- How can I be in more allowance of (me, this situation, this person)?

- What choice am I refusing to choose that if I would choose it would give me more ease, more possibility, more awareness, more joy and more choice?

- What is the value of holding onto (my worry, frustration, confusion, anger, shame, guilt, fear)?

- What am I resisting here?

- What question can I ask?

- What contribution can I be and receive (from this person, from myself)?

- What would it take for parenting to create more ease and joy in my life than I could ever possibly imagine?

- How does it get any better than this?®

- What will it take for me to destroy and uncreate this point of view?

- What am I willing to change? What am I not willing to change?

- Is this true for me?

- Who can I connect with who can give me more information?

- What would I like to have?

- What am I holding onto that if I let go of it would give me more (freedom, ease, joy etc.)?

Take a moment to write what happened. Be aware of when these situations happen. Is there a pattern? Is there a certain time of the day or situations that your kids take advantage of you and push your buttons? You can jot down anything you become aware of through these questions and this process.

_____

_____

_____

_____

_____

_____

_____

_____

_____

_____

_____

_____

_____

_____

_____

_____

_____

_____

_____

In our house, it was mealtime or when I was busy talking on the phone, that my boys would decide to push my buttons and demand my attention. In those cases asking: **"What does my child require now that I can acknowledge and change?"** You can also then ask them: **"What would it take for you to find something to do while I make dinner or finish my call?"** Simply doing this lets the child know that you acknowledge them. If they are used to you creating their possibilities, fixing their problems, dropping everything to meet their needs, then it may take them some time to get used to you asking: **What else is possible?**®

As they see you develop your question muscle and that you trust them to use theirs, they may be empowered to come up with possibilities that create more joy and fun for them too. You will find more ideas about this when we get to the creating choices section.

Another situation that seems to be a real button pusher for parents is when they are out in public with their kids. Kids know parents don't want to be judged by other people, and so they act up in public to test to see how far they can go to get what they want. If the parent gives in to their displays for public attention, whatever they are, the door has just been open for repeating the behavior. Or if you react out of anger, you have fueled a fire that may have lasting effects for you and your child.

If you are willing to let judgments go, you will find that you can ask questions from a place of non-judgment that your kids will respect. It is easier to come from a place of honor rather than fear or judgment, and you will create a better connection with your child. You will be able to ask your child what it is they really need. You will be able to let them know that their behavior doesn't work for you or for the people around you. You will be able to empower your child with questions, like **"What else might be possible for you at this moment, while I...?"** The possibilities become endless when you get out of the way and ask questions. I know it sounds rather simple, and it is. What we have made difficult about parenting is that we believe it has to be hard. The more you create an environment of allowance, without judgment, the fewer incidents you will have.

Everywhere I have bought that parenting is hard, will I destroy and uncreate all of that right now please? Right and Wrong, Good and Bad, POD and POC, All 9, Shorts, Boys and Beyonds.®

Some other questions you can use as a parent are: **"What is coming up for me in this situation?" "What does this trigger in me, that doesn't allow me to respond easily with my child?"** These questions can allow for major awareness to show up for parents as they discover they have past issues with certain behaviors.

For example a father I worked with had a daughter who was driving him nuts with her demands to be in control and causing him to become really angry. His daughter learned that if she continued to push the control buttons on her dad, he would eventually give in and give her what she wanted. Even though it wasn't what he thought was best he gave in because he was afraid of the anger he felt. As I took him through the questioning process, he became aware of how little control he had as a child. It stirred up feelings of his past that took over and didn't allow him to see what was true for him or his daughter. Using the clearing statement he began to let go of the issues of anger over not having any control in his life and began asking more questions. He was able to respond differently to his daughter and no longer became upset with her and her requests. His daughter learned she could not control her dad any longer. So ask yourself, what is coming up for you when your kids push your buttons?

One additional note on this section of button pushing: If you have identified that you need your child or your child needs you, then you have set yourself and your child up with the belief that they come before you. Even if you don't say it, your belief is transmitted energetically to your child. Being children, they will do one of two things. They will own your belief and then live according to it by being needed by you and thus taking all of your energy and time. **Or** they will do all that they can to resist the belief by pushing you away. You can't be anything for anyone else if you aren't first and foremost living your life for you! Not to worry though — as you go through these pages and practice asking questions you will get the awareness of where you are functioning from. You will be able to keep what honors you and destroy and uncreate all that doesn't.

~6~

Is This Even Mine?

"If you were being you, who would you be?"
— Dr. Dain Heer

Have you ever walked into a room and known instantly that some-thing wasn't right? You felt an anger, tension or sadness that filled the room. Or maybe it was even a joy or happiness you felt that was different than when you first came in. Well that happens a lot more than we allow ourselves to acknowledge. You see we are way more psychic than we think we are and our children are too. By psychic, I mean that we pick up other people's thoughts, feelings and emo-tions. Sometimes if we aren't aware, we think those are our thoughts, feelings and emotions. Crazy right? It is like we have an antenna that picks up all of these things, and the more the planet is feeling that way, the more we do too. We may not even know to whom they belong to, where they are or why.

I have experienced driving along the road feeling happy as a lark and then suddenly feeling mad as hell. It is interesting that our emo-tions can take control that quickly, check it out and see how often that happens to you. Not only do you experience this, but so do your kids. Becoming aware of this phenomena and knowing what to do about it can bring a lot more ease, joy and fun into life and living.

So what do we do to increase our awareness of whether these thoughts, feelings or emotions are really ours? I know it will surprise you, but simply ask either of these questions: **Is this mine?** or **Who does this belong to?**® Then follow the energy of it. What happens when you ask the question? Do you feel lighter, even just a little bit? If so, then it isn't yours. Don't get too concerned about "who" it does belong to. All you want to know is whether it is yours or not. It isn't necessary to try to figure out whom it belongs to; just acknowledging that it isn't yours is all you need to do. You can easily send it back with consciousness and ease. You can do this in any way that works for you. I just picture an envelope with wings and say, "Return to sender with awareness and ease." Done. Sometimes other people's thoughts feelings and emotions can feel like they are our own thoughts, feelings and emotions. We believe it to be so, even when they aren't. It can be helpful to add in:

Everywhere I have bought this as mine, am I willing to destroy and uncreate it? Right and Wrong, Good and Bad, POD and POC, All 9, Shorts, Boys and Beyonds.®

Also notice if you are resistant to returning the sadness, anger, fury, fear, pain or whatever else you may be experiencing back to the sender. What if by returning theses thoughts, feelings and emotions, you are offering a kindness and caring that allows them the awareness to change, if they choose?

Remember the father who was dealing with the control issues with his daughter in the last chapter? When his anger would come up he would ask the question, "Is this mine?" and found that at times the anger wasn't his. He returned it to sender and any anger that he had believed belonged to him, we cleared using the clearing statement.

Recently I was experiencing a very emotional day and I was surprised by the intensity of it. I began asking if this belonged to me. I felt lighter and so I knew it wasn't mine. I returned it to sender with consciousness and ease, and it helped knowing that it wasn't mine. Later in the day I found out that my friend's son had died that day. I had been picking up on the emotions that the mother and her family were experiencing in New Zealand. With that information I then had a choice to be sad too or not. Most of the time I don't know who the thought, feeling or emotion belongs to; I just get the sense or the knowing that it isn't mine.

As parents, you can also teach your kids to ask if what they are feeling is really theirs or someone else's. Showing them how they can return it to sender and destroy and uncreate it can also create more ease, comfort and awareness for them. Some kids are more sensitive to other people's thoughts, feelings and emotions, especially autistic kids. When you use this tool you model for them how to do it. I recall one mother at one of our workshops telling me that when she begins to react to something, her son now asks her, "Is that yours, Mom?" What a gift!

Let's practice this before moving on. Stop and check in with how you are feeling right now. It can be anything — happy, sad, stomachache, bored, angry and or hungry. Just check in and pinpoint a thought, feeling, emotion or pain you are feeling. Then ask, "Does this belong to me?" If you feel a bit of lightness — yippee, it isn't yours. Then you can package it up and send it back with consciousness and ease; in whatever way you would like to do that. Some kids like to get creative with it and blow it into a balloon and send it off, put it in an envelope with wings, or even send it back by carrier pigeon. Of course you can just send it back by simply saying the words. Now check in again and notice if you feel any difference. How long have you been buying into this issue as yours? Would you like to destroy and uncreate all of that now? Of course you can also ask more questions about it.

When you continue using these tools you will gain more aware-ness of what is really true for you. What stuff really belongs to you? Letting it go can bring a sense of freedom that many people do not experience because they are caught up in taking on other people's stuff.

 Gary Douglas recommends taking every thought, feeling and emotion that you encounter for three days and ask, **"Who does this belong to?®"** or **"Is this mine?"** and discover how much more aware you become. It works! You won't be able to do it for every thought, feeling or emotion because you will forget at times, but then you will come back to it. The more you do this, the more aware you will become, and you can stop taking on other people's stuff.

I was recently working with a client who was encountering a lot of physical discomfort. She kept thinking it was from a condition she had been diagnosed with years ago and that it kept flaring up. During a session, we found out that a lot of her pain wasn't hers and that she was just so aware of other's people's pain that she felt it too and thought it was hers. Once she started using the return to sender tool, she began to feel a lot better physically and the rest of her life changed too!

Make note of what you discovered about thoughts, feelings and emo-tions and even physical pain that you found haven't belonged to you.

_____

_____

_____

_____

_____

~7~

Choices

"Choice creates awareness."
— Gary Douglas

Now that you have learned to ask questions, how do you know what to do when possibilities show up? How do you choose from the possibilities? How do you know what is "right" for you? How do you connect with your knowing? Do you believe that you do know what is best for you? How do you help your children make choices based on their awareness?

For most of my life I didn't know that I could make choices based on what I wanted. I did what a lot of people do; I trusted everyone else to know what was right for me. Of course I did make choices, they just weren't based on asking, "What would I like to have and what would work for me?" Have you ever done the "right" thing only to have it blow up and bring you all kinds of pain, heartache and suffering, leaving you feeling smaller and smaller? I did that repeatedly. Occasionally I would be the rebel and do what I wanted to do. But because I did it out of rebelling and not out of what would work best for me, it too wouldn't work out to my advantage. Then of course I would judge myself for making "bad" or "wrong" choices. More craziness! Access Consciousness® gave me the insight to see that when I resist or react or align and agree with anything, I am not in allowance but I am in judgment. Asking a question like, "Will this work for me?" and following the energy of it means I don't have to judge or analyze to know what choice to make.

- **How can you live in peace and confidence when you are continually judging yourself?**

- **How can you discover who you really are if you are living your life to meet the standards and approval of your parents, the world, a religion, or something other than you?**

- **How do you know when to choose those things that show up as possibilities, whether they are ideas from others or things that just pop into your head?**

 Most of us aren't used to being in our awareness, and so we need a tool to help us to get in touch with our knowing. I like to use the heavy/light tool I learned from Access Consciousness®. You can use this tool for anything — making choices of any kind: what to eat, what to wear, what to do next, how to manage money, who to connect with, whether to tell your child something or not — really anything. The more you use it, the more you will get in touch with your own knowing, and before long, you will just know without cognitively using the tool. It is like having training wheels for knowing. The most difficult part is remembering that you can use it on everything.

Here's how it works. As you are making a choice, you check in and see how it feels: heavy or light? Which are you more drawn to? Most importantly, don't try to figure it out. Let your knowing come through and trust it. If you don't sense a difference and it all seems the same, ask a question, **"What would it take for me to know what is true about this?"** or **"What am I not willing to acknowledge about this that if I would acknowledge it, would allow me to know what is true for me?"**

For a long time I had trouble feeling the light and heavy sensation. For some people, it may be they see something that represents lightness or heaviness or hear a "yes" or a "no." Experiment with how your knowing communicates with you. It can be very subtle. After a while of sticking with it, I now have a better sense of the light and heavy.

"If it feels light, it is true. If it feels heavy, it is a lie. This one tool will give you the ability to follow the energy of what will expand your life for everything you are choosing."
— Gary Douglas

The choices you make while using the light and heavy tool may not make sense at the time because your mind wants to analyze, compute and compare to make a decision. Following the light or heavy feeling takes you away from cognitive thinking. This allows you to follow an energetic flow and ease that often brings about choices that you could never think of in your cognitive mind. What feels light is true for you, what is heavy is most likely a lie, or you have a judgment about it that doesn't let you acknowledge the truth.

Imagine empowering your children with this tool! It will give you much more ease knowing they know how to choose based upon their knowing. Play with it and see what changes.

What are some things that you can begin to use for Light and Heavy? Making a list of things may help you trigger the memory to remember to check in. Start with easy things, like your choices for what you are going to wear, which direction to turn or which route to travel, what to have to eat, which activity to do, whether to tell your child something or not (there may be a better time later). As you go through your day be aware of how many choices you make in a day. For each of those, you could be using "Light and Heavy" to help you choose and take the stress out of making choices. The stress comes from the judgment of having to make the "right" choice. Remember, there are no right or wrong choices — just choices.

_____

_____

_____

_____

_____

_____

_____

_____

_____

_____

A couple of alternatives to light and heavy that some people prefer is to ask "yes" or "no," and sense which one shows up first without any thought. An example would be, "Turn right at the corner?" Yes or No? Or, "Have sweet potatoes for dinner?" Yes or No? And I have friends who use muscle testing as a way of accessing the same information as light and heavy. A simple way to do that is to stand with your feet together and say, "Yes" and see what your body does. It will tend to sway in one direction. Then say, "No" and see what direction your body sways. There can be factors that can affect your results, so if this is of interest to you ask some questions about who you can connect with to learn more about muscle testing.

You can use Light and Heavy for anything. The key is to trust your knowing without analyzing or needing to know why. It is through choosing that you will become more aware.

When you notice that you have forgotten to use a tool — such as asking a question or checking in with heavy or light, don't make yourself wrong for it just notice and ask: **"What would it take for me to remember to use the tools more often?"** It takes time to get into the practice. I know people — myself included — who have been using these tools for many years and forget to use them. What I notice for myself is that when I do forget, I acknowledge that I could have done something different and I chose not to. I move on with new awareness and leave the judgment behind. Life is so much more fun when we stop judging everything we do or don't do.

Everywhere I am trying and trying to do the right thing so I can continue to judge myself, will I destroy and uncreate all of that now please?

Right and Wrong, Good and Bad, POD and POC, All 9, Shorts, Boys and Beyonds.®

What if having children could be a part of creating an extraordinary life?

I wonder if that would be a question worth asking. Being a parent is always a choice and your children have chosen you as their parents. Being in a place of choice eliminates feeling trapped as a parent. Your points of view create everything in your life. How much lighter would you feel if you knew that your points of view also included the parents you chose to have? What if you were part of their extraordinary life?

I often get asked what parents can do when their kids make choices that aren't in their best interest? How can parents empower their kids to make better choices? When choices don't work out you can simply let your children know they can choose something else. Also a choice may work for a while, and then after some time it might stop working. What if you could give yourself permission to make a different choice? There seems to be a limiting belief that once you make a "decision," you have to stick by it no matter what. Do you sense a difference in the words "Decision" and "Choice"? The word *decide,* is from the Latin, to cut off, to separate and the word choice is from the Latin, to examine.[1] Which feels lighter to you? Have you been making decisions that have cut you off from having more possibilities because you lock yourself into your decision believing that it can't be changed? Who does that belong to? A belief like this may leave a person feeling trapped. When making choices, you can always make a different choice whenever you like. What if you apply the same concept to when your child makes a choice that doesn't go as they thought it would? Are you going to require them to keep doing something just because they chose it and then found out that they didn't enjoy what they chose?

Consider Courtney, a curious and active seven year old. She loves to experience new things. Her mother signs her up for tap dance class and after 2 classes Courtney doesn't want to go any more. She now wants to take a class in country dancing. So her mother now signs her daughter up for country dancing class. After a class or two, Courtney wants to try jazz dancing. And so the classes keep coming. What could Courtney's mother do in this situation? She could force her daughter to stick to the choices she made, telling her that once you make a decision, you need to stick with it. How does that feel? What would Courtney learn from that? Would that response allow Courtney more ease in choice or less? OR is there another response Courtney's mother could have? She could be happy allowing Courtney to change classes until she finds the one that she likes or just exposes her to them as a matter of information. If she finds that it doesn't work for her to keep signing up for classes, she may ask some questions. "What do I know about Courtney that will assist me in this situation?" "How can I contribute to Courtney's desire to know what she would like?" "What else is possible?" The mother may discover that she knows that her daughter is curious and wants to experience many things. She might then ask, "What would it

---

[1] Webster's *Revised Unabridged Dictionary* (1913 + 1828)

take to allow Courtney to have experiences that work for me also?" Perhaps she will "stumble" onto some other possibilities that work for both of them. She may even be able to include Courtney in how to make choices by together asking questions that allow her daughter to be able to connect to her knowing. It is in asking questions and being in allowance that will create infinite possibilities to come forth from which to choose.

When you allow your kids to make choices for themselves you allow them to discover what works in their life for them, and this helps them develop their sense of awareness. You will lose your credibility with your child if you tell her what you think will happen if she does something, and she goes ahead and does it and nothing happens. This is also how parents instill fear in their children. Using questions when your child wants to do something that you sense may be harmful will be more helpful as they will get a sense of what the outcome may be.

- **Where can you give your children more choice and be in allowance of their choices?**

- **What if you didn't judge their choices as right or wrong but just as choices?**

And everything that brings up, will I destroy and uncreate all of that? Right and Wrong, Good and Bad, POD and POC, All 9, Shorts, Boys and Beyonds.®

Here is an example. Carrie wants to ride her bike but she doesn't want to wear her helmet.

First ASK if there is a reason she doesn't want to wear her helmet? Kids often won't volunteer the reasons unless you ask. Maybe the helmet is too small and hurts her head, or maybe she has trouble seeing when wearing the helmet. She may have a legitimate reason. **Listen and acknowledge.** Avoid discounting their reasons. If your child believes you're not listening to them they may stop communicating with you. It is rare that children just do not want to do something, although it may seem that way because no one has ever asked.

Let's say you have taken care of any issue around the helmet and she still doesn't want to wear it. You can continue asking questions about safety. *What are you aware of here? Would wearing your helmet help your body?* As you ask questions, allow the child to see what is possible. Some parents will project fear with such situations by telling the child that if they don't wear their helmet they could fall and hurt themselves. And while this may be a possibility, would you rather have your child live in awareness by asking questions or in fear of what might happen?

You can compare it to why you wear your seat belt. What if you talk to you kid about what a seat belt or helmet does? What if by knowing what it can do for them would allow them to make a more informed choice? Often when kids know what things are for instead of you just imposing your will on them, they are more than happy to give their body extra protection. When you allow your kids to make their own choices, they feel empowered. They know you trust them to make choices that are in their best interest. They also know you will be there for them if their choices don't work out as they had planned. It is called choosing and becoming aware.

I recall a boy sharing with me that his parents were always complaining to him that he wouldn't brush his teeth at bedtime. No one ever asked him why he didn't brush his teeth; they just assumed he was too lazy or just forgot. When I asked him, he said he didn't like to go to bed with the taste of toothpaste in his mouth. Then I asked him if there would be another time that he could brush his teeth that would solve that issue? He simply said that he could brush right after dinner, since he didn't usually eat anything else at night, that way by the time he went to bed the taste of toothpaste would be out of his mouth. He did this and it wasn't a problem anymore.

When you have difficulty allowing your child to make choices, you might ask yourself:

"What is this bringing up in me?"

"Do I trust myself to make my own choices?"

"How much have I judged my past choices?"

"Am I ready to destroy and uncreate all of those judgments?"

Asking these questions as well as any question you ask your child is more empowering when you don't have a point of view about the question or the response. When you have a reaction to something your child does or says, it may be a reflection of what you are projecting, and your child is picking up on it and mirroring it back to you. It is a wonderful opportunity for you to gain insight into what is really going on for you. It may also be a time to pull out your tools to discover what issues you have coming up that you feel the urge to project your point of view onto your child.

- **Are you afraid to allow your child to make choices, because you weren't allowed to make your choices when you were a child?**

- **Are you afraid that your child's choices will turn out the same way that yours did?**

- **Are you afraid to let your child experience struggle, failure, disappointment, or even success?**

- **Do you find it difficult to believe in your child when no one even you believed in you as a child?**

These are some issues that have come up with parents I have known. I appreciate the courage and willingness it takes to face these beliefs. We have to become honest with ourselves if we are going to change. But now you have tools to apply so that your limiting beliefs and judgments won't stop you from being you. You can now eliminate them and be more of you. Begin with asking, "Who does that belong to?" Then you can destroy and uncreate any fixed points of view that you have from your own experiences or beliefs. Continue to ask questions of yourself to have more clarity around any issue. Let go of any urge to have it all "fixed" right now. Be patient with the process. You'll get it when you get it and it will all be just what you required.

Allowing your child to make choices does not mean you allow them to make choices that don't work for you. This is not about letting your kids walk all over you. There is a distinction between honoring yourself and allowing your kids to choose. I encourage you to look at what motivates you to choose for your kids. What if you asked your kids what they would like to choose? When your children are making choices, let them know if a choice won't work for you at the time. If it is a case that the child wants to do something that you aren't willing to have them do, ask them: "What else is possible?"

Have you ever noticed what happens when you tell your child "No?" Does he resist you more and put more effort into getting you to say yes? Letting him know that what he is asking for doesn't work for you right now, and asking him if something else may be possible, removes the "No" from the equation and allows him to consider something else. It is another way of empowering your child. You may also find that it is easier for you. You won't have to put out as much energy to put up a fight about something that can easily be addressed with questions. I would like to emphasize again here that communicating with your child without any judgment or fixed point of view will allow this to happen with ease and joy.

For an example, let's say Grant wants you to buy him a new toy at the store and it is not in your budget. You can let Grant know that at this time the toy doesn't fit into your budget. Then you can let him know that when you want to buy something and you don't have the money for it yet, you ask questions like:

"What would it take to have the money to buy this toy?"

"It isn't in my budget to buy this toy today; I wonder what else is possible?"

What if you could...

- **Share these tools with your kids?**

- **Teach them to ask and receive by sharing your experiences?**

- **Offer them alternative choices?**

What choices am I refusing to allow my children to make that if I would be in total allowance would give them and me total choice, joy and ease? Everything that brings up, will I destroy and uncreate it all? Right and Wrong, Good and Bad, POD and POC, All 9, Shorts, Boys and Beyonds.®

Imagine not judging your choices?

One mother told me she knew having kids would keep her from being the free spirit she longed to be. And yet she found herself agreeing to be married with kids because she thought since it seemed to work for others perhaps she too could find happiness as a wife and mother. After a few years she became depressed, being torn between her kids whom she cared for dearly, and a way of life that allowed her to be able to move about from place to place. After learning these tools, she is discovering that there are ways that she can have both. It doesn't look like the other families she knows and she faces judgment from others but she is becoming more of who she is and her kids have a mother who is working on her own happiness. She inspires me with her willingness to create a life that is beyond what she ever thought possible.

I have met other parents who regret having children. They tell me this isn't what they signed up for and they find the job of parenting cramps their lifestyle and is simply too challenging. This point of view, however, does not take into consideration that they chose to be a parent for whatever reason. Here are some questions to allow the person to gain more clarity.

- **What is right about this that I am not willing to acknowledge?**

- **Is there something here that I can learn about myself?**

- **What can I gain from this experience that I never thought possible?**

- **What would it take for me to be in allowance of myself, and my child?**

- **What would make this easier for both of us?**

- **What would it take for my children to be a contribution to my life?**

- **What else is possible that I never even considered?**

Whether or not you are a parent, life presents challenges. These challenges are based upon our own points of view. If you change your point of view, you can change your reality. Then your challenges turn into opportunities and awareness. Keep in mind that you did choose to be a parent, and whatever challenges you are having, it all has a purpose. It is not for me to judge how you handle them, just to offer tools that may create a different possibility.

Before we move on, one more comment on the choices your kids make.

Would you be willing to *not* judge you for the choices your child makes?

Whether they make good choices or bad choices, would you be willing to let your kids have full credit? Children are beings in little bodies, and they too have choice and will create their lives based on their points of view. It is not that you can't teach them anything about life, but know that they will develop their own perception based on how they are judged or not judged. Sharing these tools and techniques with them will help them be aware of what is in their best interest. It isn't necessary to force the tools onto your kids. You can offer them as possibilities. A simple way to do this is to say something like, *"I wonder if that anger belongs to you."* Or *"I wonder if something else is possible that we haven't thought of yet. What do you think?"* Ease into sharing the tools, apply them to your life, be willing to openly use them in front of your kids for yourself, and allow them to see what difference it makes in your life. All too often people see the benefit of these tools. Then they want to tell all of their friends as well as their kids that they too need to be doing these things. That kind of force is usually met with resistance. If you know that you being you is all that is required to offer the possibility of change to others — it may be received with more ease. People will want to know what you are doing and then you can let them know.

Everywhere I have made it my job to fix other people's lives rather than creating more possibility and choice for myself will I destroy and uncreate all of that? Right and Wrong, Good and Bad, POD and POC, All 9, Shorts, Boys and Beyonds.®

There is another fear that some parents have with regards to their children — fear that their child's choice may get the child into trouble with the law. If your child gets into trouble that lands them in jail or the court system does it mean you are a bad parent? The first time one of my sons got into trouble for stealing, I felt that I must be the worst parent in the world. (Be sure to read the chapter on guilt too.) I didn't realize how destructive judging both of us would be. It created a distance between the two of us for a period of time. I didn't have the tools to empower both of us by asking questions, being in allowance and trusting him to make a different choice. I have since destroyed and uncreated all of the judgments, mistrust and anger I had about that situation.

Fortunately, I was more aware when my youngest son ended up in jail. I was able to choose how I could contribute in a way that would honor both of us. I found it easy not to judge him, to allow and trust him to figure out what other possibilities he had to choose from. This experience allowed him to come to his own awareness about his life and what he could change. He has been empowered through this experience and has become more of who he can be. I would deny him that experience for what reason?

I have a good friend who let her son sit in jail after his DUI, and he stayed there through Thanksgiving. I know it was really difficult for the parent to do this, but she also knew that by doing so, she was letting him choose what he wanted to do with this situation. Some parents may think she abandoned him, but in truth, she did the best thing she could to support him. He knew she cared about him and that she would be there for him when he made his choice of what to do next. He also knew that she wasn't judging him for the situation he had gotten himself into. She had let go of any fear of being judged by others; knowing that the best way to support and parent him was to let him create his own life.

How many of us have made choices that didn't work out the way we thought they would and were even embarrassed by them? How much did your life change because of those choices? Did those choices give you an awareness and information of how you wanted to live your life? Your choices are what give you awareness; they teach you about yourself. My son learned from his choices what was missing in his life, and how he was letting his past effect his present way of living. The sooner you allow your kids to have choices, the sooner they will have the awareness and knowing of who they are. The gift you give them is in allowing them to make choices without your judgment. Ask yourself: how would it feel for you not to be judged for your choices?

In addition when you see your child headed toward a dangerous choice, like jumping off a cliff, you might ask them some questions about what might happen if he or she chooses that? Is that the only choice? What else is possible? If you choose this what will your life be like in 5 years, 10 years? What will the world be like in 500 years? If you don't choose this what will your life be like in 5 years, 10 years? What will the world be like in 500 years? Does the choice feel light or heavy? You **cannot** control them and empower them at the same time.

Did you notice that we added in the future as well as the effect the choice will make for the world? What if the choices we make today, impact our future — 5 even 10 years or more from now? Wouldn't we want to tap into the energy of that in order to make choices that will contribute to our future? AND what if the choices we make today impact the future of our planet, our world? Imagine your kids making choices now that also contribute to their future and the world.

 Take a moment to ask questions about choices. Remember that you aren't looking to come up with an answer. Just allow the insights to show up and you'll know.

- **What choices am I refusing to choose that if I would choose them would give me total choice?**

- **Where do I notice resistance to making choices?**

- **What choices am I not allowing my child to make?**

- **For what reason would I stop my child from making his or her own choices?**

- **Am I afraid of being judged for the choices my child makes?**

- **How right do I need to be about my choices?**

- **What would my life be like if I didn't judge my choices?**

With these questions notice what comes up, along with any questions you may have of your own. Ask what tool you might use to apply to those questions to open things up for more awareness and change. Will you destroy and uncreate it? Will you apply the clearing statement to it? Will you ask, "Who does that belong to?" Or will you ask more questions? The choice is yours, and by making a choice you will have more awareness.

You may want to make some notes here on how this is working
for you.

_____

_____
_____
_____
_____
_____
_____
_____
_____
_____
_____
_____
_____
_____
_____
_____
_____
_____
_____
_____
_____
_____
_____
_____
_____
_____
_____
_____

~8~

Motivate Through Acknowledgement

"Knowledge is in the end based on what is acknowledged."
— Ludwig Wittgenstein

 Acknowledgement is the method that has been proven to promote more motivation for kids and for people of all ages. Acknowledgement is used to replace praise and compliments in many cases.

Mattison Grey and Jonathan Manske tell us in their book, *The Motivation Myth:*

"Acknowledgement effectively conveys attention, appreciation, being valued, and your belief in another person. These are the things that people crave. They get the message that they matter and that you get them."

We have been trained to compliment our kids to encourage them to continue to do the things we have decided are good and to discourage them from the things we have judged as bad.

Let's take a look.

Think of the last time you complimented your child. What did you say? Write down a few examples.

_____

_____

_____

_____

_____

_____

_____

_____

_____

_____

_____

_____

_____

_____

Here are some I hear and have used myself:

"I am so proud of you for getting an A on your test."

"It makes me happy that you cleaned up your room."

"What a great job you did on your homework."

What do you notice about these statements? Do they acknowledge or judge? Are they about the person or about you? When we compliment we include judgments and our points of view. These do not allow the person to receive a true acknowledgement of what they have done. It trains our kids to look for receiving judgments rather than awareness as their guide for knowing how to choose. It also teaches them that judgments are more important than acknowledgements.

The key components to acknowledgement include:

- **What was actually done or accomplished.**

- **Be specific.**

- **Something that is completed.**

- **Keep it short.**

- **Only one thing at a time — don't lump them all together, it gets blurred.**

- **Listen to what they say to know what to acknowledge**

- **Leave "you" out of it.**

- **No adjectives or modifiers — they add your judgment to the statement.**

- **Acknowledge individuals not groups.**

- **Put your energy behind your acknowledgement.**

Examples:

♥ You got an A on the test!

♥ You cleaned your room.

♥ You finished your homework.

♥ You got ready for bed on time.

When children hear these types of statements, they will go inside and repeat that, yes, **they** did get an A on test, **they** did clean their room, and **they** did get ready for bed on time. This reinforces what they know.

Now go back to the compliments you wrote down above and see how you can turn them into acknowledgments. This doesn't mean you will never compliment your child. Instead what would your relationship be like if you did more acknowledging and offered a compliment here and there? These acknowledgments will empower your child to know that he or she is capable and successful and can achieve. In other words, they will begin to believe and trust themselves more and more. See how your child responds to being acknowledged. Give them several opportunities to experience being acknowledged for their own awareness. Most children have been programmed to look for praise and have come to value it as a way of acknowledging themselves. Your child may feel like it is weird and may not be sure how to process it. My sense is that we all want to be acknowledged for what we do without judgment, and that it is worth the effort to impart statements of acknowledgment.

You can also use the acknowledgement strategy for times when your child doesn't follow through on something. Instead of "I am so disappointed that you forgot to turn in your homework." You could just say, "You forgot to turn in your homework." And if it seems the time to add a question, you might add, "What else is possible to change that?"

What would happen if you acknowledged more of what you have accomplished? Would you get a better sense of you? Would you be more appreciative of your talents and abilities? Keep an acknowledgment journal by your bedside. Each night before you go to sleep, write down 3–5 things you can acknowledge yourself for doing that day. Be aware of what comes up for you as you do this. Is it easy for you to give yourself credit?

When I first started doing this exercise, I discovered that it was difficult for me to give acknowledgement for myself. It felt very uncomfortable and yet I knew it would be helpful for me. So I asked, "What is this? What do I do with this? Can I change it? If so how?" Remember these 4 questions? The awareness that came was that ever since I was a child, everything I did was to gain acceptance and acknowledgement from my parents, teachers and other adults. I didn't do anything for me. I kept looking for that praise — even at the age of 50! Once I got that awareness, I was able to destroy and uncreate all of it and choose to acknowledge my gifts and talents and being. If you find it difficult to do this exercise, you may find some awareness around asking questions.

Everywhere I keep looking to others to acknowledge me and my value, will I destroy and uncreate all of that? Right and Wrong, Good and Bad, POD and POC, All 9, Shorts, Boys and Beyonds.®

Everywhere I avoid acknowledging myself in order to keep myself small and meaningless, will I destroy and uncreate all of that? Right and Wrong, Good and Bad, POD and POC, All 9, Shorts, Boys and Beyonds.®

- **What would it take for me to acknowledge my own greatness?**

- **What do I know about myself, that if I would acknowledge my knowing, I would be able to be more of who I truly BE?**

Do you find yourself making excuses for how amazing you are? You may find more opportunities to destroy and uncreate whatever comes up. I would also bet that most of what you discover, if not all, doesn't belong to you either. Owning your own greatness will show your kids how to be in their greatness too. The world requires you to be all that you are here to be. That is you being the greatness you are. It isn't about comparing yourself to others. It is about stopping the self-judgment and stepping more into acknowledging all that you be.

I highly recommend the book *The Motivation Myth,* by Mattison Grey and Jonathan Manske to learn more about this strategy.

What If Worry and Fear Didn't Exist?

"Our fatigue is often caused not by work, but by worry, frustration and resentment."
— Dale Carnegie

- **What would it take to be a parent without fear, worry or sleepless nights?**

- **What would that be like?**

- **Would it be different than what you are creating now?**

- **What would your children generate if you were not afraid for them, if they were not afraid, and if they actually had access to what they know?**

Worry is steeped in fear, fear of the unknown.

I can remember countless nights lying awake wondering if my kids would be okay. I would lay awake waiting for them to come in from evenings with friends. I would lay awake wondering if they would be able to resolve their issues or if there was something I needed to do to make life better for them. I would lay awake wondering what our futures held. Would I have enough money to provide for them? How many sleepless nights and endless days do you encounter worrying and fretting? Has any of that worrying changed anything or made life better? Do you tend to worry about everyone else too? Have you taken on a belief that if you don't worry about your kids it means that you don't love or care about them? Who does that belong to? What if not worrying about your kids actually empowers them?

Are your kids better off because you worry about them? What is the underlying cause of your worry? What are you aware of that if you asked more questions would allow you to know all that you need to know? How does it get any better than this?

What does it take to stop worrying about your kids? Here are some tips:

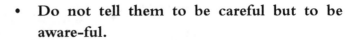 • **Do not tell them to be careful but to be aware-ful.**

When you tell your children to be careful, it projects that there is danger out there, which may or may not be the case. It doesn't allow for the child to be aware and to follow their awareness by asking questions. Telling your kids to be "careful" projects a fear of the unknown. Do you want your children to live in the fear of what might happen or be empowered to be aware of what is happening? Teach your children that when something doesn't feel right to ask a question that will empower them to access their own knowing.

"If I choose this what will my life be like in 5 years, 10 years? What will the world be like in 500 years?" Light or Heavy?

"If I don't choose this what will my life be like in 5 years, 10 years? What will the world be like in 500 years?" Light or Heavy?

Are you willing to be judged as a bad parent?

By this, I mean are you willing to be different from other parents? Don't let the fact that others may judge you keep you from parenting from your awareness. It may, and most probably will, be different than the way others parent. I would suggest you find other parents who honor conscious parenting and support each other in asking questions, choosing and being in allowance.

Allowing your children to create their own life is not a bad thing. It is the way that you empower your children to learn from their own experiences. This will reduce and maybe even eliminate the worry. When you find yourself pulling back because you are afraid of what others will say, ask if this is: "Yours or someone else's?" and then destroy and uncreate all those areas where you fear being judged. Set the picture of your empowered kids in front of you. Let that be your target and focus. Can you perceive that this will make a difference in your life?

Everywhere I am refusing to parent from a place of being willing to be judged, will I destroy and uncreate that? Right and Wrong, Good and Bad, POD and POC, All 9, Shorts, Boys and Beyonds.®

- **Fear is always a distraction from awareness. Ask a question.**

Recognize that when you are fearful and worried you are not being aware. Asking a question, finding and stating gratitude, and acknowledging that something is going on will give you the knowing of what to do next. If you don't destroy and uncreate that fear could you be preventing yourself from experiencing something else, like ease and joy?

- **Is my child safe?**

- **What am I aware of?**

- **Is this mine?**

- **What does my child know that I am not aware of?**

Asking these questions will give you the knowing of whether your child is truly safe or not. If you ask, "Is my child safe?" and you get a sinking, heavy feeling, then ask another question. Don't freak out, as that will not allow you to receive what you need to know. Ask: "What else do I need to know or do?" "What is this that I am aware of?" "Is this mine?" You can also include: "What does my child know that I am not aware of?" This will allow you to key into their awareness also. Just keep asking, and you will know if you need to take action or not. In this day of cell phones, it is easy to text your child or call them to just check in with a quick question. It is wise to let your child know that, in addition to them being aware, that you continue to use your awareness too. It is not about not trusting them, but rather connecting to your awareness and knowing.

As parents we seem to inherit a mega-ton of fear about our kids from the start. Inherit is the correct word as we are not the originators of our fears. They have been thoughts and beliefs we have picked up throughout our lifetimes. How many times did your parents tell you to "Watch out?" There are numerous "old wives tales" that parents use to instill fear into their kids. How many remember hearing their mothers say, "If you don't wear your coat, you will catch a cold." I have known many kids who don't wear coats and don't get sick, and there are kids who, regardless of what they wear, get sick. What if you asked your kids, "Would you like to take your coat in case you get cold?" When we ask our kids and let them choose, it demonstrates to them that we trust them to make choices that work for them, even if it isn't what we would choose. If your child questions you, then he will test your theories and when he finds out they aren't true for him he won't believe anything you say.

Many of our fears also come from the fear that our children will fall into the same traps we fell into, so we project our fears onto them. What were your experiences growing up that you regret? Are they things you are afraid your children will experience? Even if they do, will their outcomes be the same as yours? Watching a child climb a tree, many parents would say something like, "Come down before you break a bone." This instills in the child that they need to be afraid. Instead you might ask, "Are you having fun? What do you know? What do you sense about this?" There are many kids who are expert climbers and simply have no fear. They usually have more fun. Sometimes a broken bone, bruised knee or burnt finger is the way they will gain the awareness for themselves. In the cases when they do experience physical pain are you the parent that says: "I told you so"? Or are you in total allowance and allow them to gain awareness from their choices?

There are parents that would like to always be right about everything. They have a fear about being wrong. These parents have something that they need to prove about themselves. They hold beliefs about being wrong, that requires them to prove that they are right. Some kids can do the same thing. Rather than make another choice that would work out better, these beings continue to choose in order to prove themselves right. How well is that working for anyone? Does that feel heavy or light?

If you don't have to prove anything, does it allow more ease to choose?

Everywhere I am making myself wrong in order to be right, and right in order to be wrong that keeps me from having infinite choice, will I destroy and uncreate all of that? Right and Wrong, Good and Bad, POD and POC, All 9, Shorts, Boys and Beyonds.®

All the fears I have about being right or wrong will I destroy and uncreate all of that now please? Right and Wrong, Good and Bad, POD and POC, All 9, Shorts, Boys and Beyonds.®

In order to tackle the issue of fear, it can be helpful to acknowledge what you are afraid of, especially in connection to your kids. Take a moment and write down some of your fears and worries:

_____

_____

_____

_____

_____

_____

_____

_____

_____

_____

_____

_____

_____

_____

_____

_____

_____

 Here are a few steps I learned from Dr. Dain Heer that you can use to help remove those fears: (Be sure to ask "Truth" with all of your questions. If you aren't completely honest with yourself, you won't be able to get past the fear.)

1. Ask the question, is this fear really mine?

2. If it isn't yours, set it free and return to sender.

3. If it is yours, begin to acknowledge that it is yours and what would it take to get rid of it so it no longer distracts you from your choice and awareness?

All of the fears I have about (insert your fear), will I destroy and uncreate them all now? Right and Wrong, Good and Bad, POD and POC, All 9, Shorts, Boys and Beyonds.®

4. What is really true about this? Fear is a lie you have bought somewhere, and the sooner you discover what is really true for you, the sooner you can let go of the fear. Fear is a projection of what might happen and you have bought it as what will happen?

All of the lies that I have bought that are creating this fear, will I destroy and uncreate them all now? Right and Wrong, Good and Bad, POD and POC, All 9, Shorts, Boys and Beyonds.®

Everything that doesn't allow me to see the truth in all of this, will I destroy and uncreate all of that? Right and Wrong, Good and Bad, POD and POC, All 9, Shorts, Boys and Beyonds.®

5. Destroy and uncreate all the places where you are allowing fear to distract you from having all of you. How much is fear getting in the way of having what you would really like to have? How much is fear getting in the way of you BEING YOU? What would life be like for you and your children if you didn't live in fear?

All distractors of fear that I have running, will I destroy and uncreate them all now? Right and Wrong, Good and Bad, POD and POC, All 9, Shorts, Boys and Beyonds.®

You might also ask:

- **Do I have a need that I am not willing to let go of?**

- **Is my need for my child so strong that I fear losing him? Of not being needed?**

- **Am I holding onto something that isn't mine?**

Let's consider these last two questions. Naturally parents would like their kids to have long and happy lives. However, parents are not in control and to think they can be sets up a misconception. Children are not possessions, even though you pay the bills. They have a life of their own and will move through this lifetime much easier if they are given the choice to choose the life they desire for as long as they choose to live it. Just as you and I have the same choices and would not want anyone to tell us differently. Your role is to give them the tools to create possibilities from which to choose. There are infinite possibilities, so they always have choices to choose from.

I thought my children belonged to me. I gave them life, I cared for them and I certainly knew what was best for them based on my experiences. I had my first son when I was a teen and married his father and we divorced a few years later. I remarried and wanted so badly to have a family life that seemed more like the family that I grew up with — you know — perfect. So when my middle son Ben came along, I wanted to do everything "right" by him. For me, that meant I would stay at home and take care of him. I would make all the "right" choices for him and for his schooling. I would take control so that he got everything that he needed. All this was based on what I had heard from others who I thought knew better than me how to raise my child, you know who they are — the church leaders, the doctors, the therapists, the teachers, and other experts.

As part of making sure his life went well, I began to force these beliefs onto him, and he didn't like it very much. He would refuse to participate in church activities and family activities. At that time I didn't know much about asking kids questions. I believed I was supposed to know what was right and good for each of them. After all, I had turned to the adults in my life growing up to tell me what to do and how to live my life. If I had paid more attention to choosing what would make me happy, I could have shown my kids that they could choose the things in life that would work to their advantage. Letting others tell me what to choose did not allow me to learn how to make choices for me that would contribute to my life. I did not have the confidence to know what I really wanted from life at that time. I had bought into the idea that being a parent and having a family was the most important thing a person could be or do. I felt that I had to know it all in order to help my sons. I can really see how if I had known how to use questions and choice, I could have made some different choices.

Ben was sensitive to others and picked up on their sadness. He took it on as his job to make others happy. He struggled with being happy. I wonder if he didn't also sense that no matter how hard he tried to make others happy, their own sadness and turmoil continued. This inner struggle continued for Ben, until at the age of 19 he ended his life by his own hand. In that moment, my life changed irrevocably. Nothing would be the same ever again, and that became the catalyst for changing my life.

After Ben died, I began to question all of the beliefs that I had up to that point. It became an ardent quest of mine to connect to the truth of why am I here, what is my purpose, and what am I supposed to do now? I learned that I was not in control of Ben's life; I wasn't even in control of my own life. I began to let go. In doing so I allowed Ben to have his life and his death as his choice. I found gratitude for all he gave to me in both life and death.

At some point in this process of discovery, an Access Consciousness® facilitator asked me if I was an infinite being. I wasn't sure in that moment what that meant, but it gave me a lightness that I couldn't ignore. As I asked questions around it, I became aware that being an infinite being means that there is no beginning or end to my being. If I expand out my energy in all directions; there is no end to me. Acknowledging that I am infinite being means that although I have this body, which allows me to be in this physical space, I am not limited by it. And when this body ends its existence here, I the being still exist and always will. And as infinite beings, death does not end our connection with one another. In some cases, when we allow it to, it deepens and we continue to contribute to each other's existence. I let go of the fear I had about my remaining loved ones, and stepped into the knowing that we all are given free will to live and die as we choose.

To live in fear of losing our children makes it more difficult for them to live fully as the infinite beings that they be. To hold your children bound to you through need does not allow you or them to be all that you both can be. Your role as parent is not to hold them to you but to show them how to fly, wherever that may be.

Ben's life and death have given me more freedom to be me without living in fear, worry, guilt, blame or doubt. I now know what it means to LIVE as I have never lived before — as ME. I am full of gratitude for what Ben has given me and what I have given him through my own transformation. And that transformation continues for both of us as we continue to step into more awareness and consciousness.

When you live in fear, you lose trust in yourself, and you show your kids that they can't trust you or themselves. You project fear onto your kids they normally wouldn't have. And until they learn to question whether the fear is theirs or not, they may believe it is theirs and live their life from that fear. How much of your fear has been projected onto you from your childhood?

All of the fear I that I took on as a child that keeps me from truly living, will I destroy and uncreate all of that? Right and Wrong, Good and Bad, POD and POC, All 9, Shorts, Boys and Beyonds.®

All of the fear I carry about — whether my child will live or die — that actually keeps me, and my child from truly living, will I destroy and uncreate all of that? Right and Wrong, Good and Bad, POD and POC, All 9, Shorts, Boys and Beyonds.®

Additionally, I have learned that it is not our job as parents to make our kids happy. It is our job to allow them to choose to be happy if they so desire it and not make them wrong if they choose to not be happy. It is our job to let them know that there may be another choice, if they would like to explore that by asking a question. How many people do you know who aren't happy? Yet they seem to be fine with not being happy because they aren't doing anything to change it. Judging our lives by how happy we are is still living in judgment. What if happiness is just a choice? What if children learn that happiness is a choice they can choose anytime they wish? What if children learn that choosing something else can change anything that isn't working for them? Most kids come into this world with a desire to be happy. Most kids know the purpose of life is to live in joy and happiness. That is until they are told to be serious, to be quiet, to take the fun someplace else and to limit themselves by not being seen. What would it take to destroy and uncreate all of that?

Make additional notes about fear here:

_____

_____

~10~

Allowance

"Consciousness is the ability to be present in your life in every moment, without judgment of you or anyone else. It is the ability to receive everything, reject nothing, and create everything you desire in life — greater than what you currently have, and more than what you can imagine."
— Gary Douglas

Being willing to be more conscious as a parent means being willing to be in more allowance as a parent. We have actually been talking about this throughout the book. But let's take some time to look specifically at allowance. By allowance I don't mean how much money you give your kids for weekly chores. In this instance, allowance means to be out of judgment of yourself and your kids. We all make choices, we all have points of view and we all do things that don't always go the way we thought they would. What if none of that had to be judged? What if we just acknowledged it as a choice and asked questions?

Being in allowance of your kids, does not mean they get everything they want. It does mean that you listen, you be aware, you ask questions and you never judge them. It also means that when they are making a choice that involves you, you do have a say about it. Be willing to know what works for you and let your children know that. You can honor yourself without having to dishonor your children. When you have a nurturing and caring response to your kids' requests, they will learn that you take care of yourself by voicing your desires. Having allowance for your children does not mean being a doormat or putting up with what does not work for you. One of the greatest gifts we give our kids is showing them how to honor ourselves first.

In a recent workshop a parent asked about being in allowance of letting her kids watch too much TV. My question about that would be: What judgments do you have about "too much TV" that you may be projecting onto your kids? Also, how do you let your kids know there are other ways to have fun in life? What if you asked what else is possible as far as different ways to spend their time? It might also be beneficial to find out what they find so entertaining about watching hours of TV. If you don't make it about a judgment such as: "Too much TV is bad for you." And you make it more about, "What else is there that you can do that would be fun?" You empower your kids to discover more about what else is possible. They won't have to align and agree with your judgment or resist and react to it. TV just becomes a choice. How many times have you as a parent watched TV and then had the awareness that you could have spent your time in a different way that may have been a better use of your time? What if we let our kids know that we always have the choice to make a different choice by sharing with them what we discover? An example might be: "Last night I stayed up late watching a movie and today I am tired. Next time I choose to watch TV, I will check in with my body and see if it feels like staying up that late. I will ask, 'If I choose this what will my life be like?'"

Children are master manipulators; there is nothing wrong with this. You do get to choose when to allow them to manipulate you or not.

Ask: Truth is this child manipulating me?

Yes, okay fine, I am willing to do that for them. Or no, that doesn't work for me. Then rather than telling them "No," let them know that at this time you can't do what they want. And is there something else they would like to do instead? This leaves room for something different that will work for both of you.

 Be the energy that is required in each situation to change it, even if that means being fierce. When a parent uses the energy of fierceness or softness, it is always without judgment. It is not the same as using anger to control. It is used to let our kids know that we mean what we say. You may ask, **"What energy is required of me at this time with this person?"**

What energy am I refusing to be that would allow me to handle this situation with ease and joy? Everything that doesn't allow me to be the energy that is required, will I destroy and uncreate all of that now? Right and Wrong, Good and Bad, POD and POC, All 9, Shorts, Boys and Beyonds.®

When you are in allowance, it means you are not controlling your children. Many parents use anger as a way to control and instill fear in their kids. This is not allowance, and issues around anger require questions. Anger is like fear in that it distracts us from being aware and in our knowing. When the tools are used, a person can eliminate anger from his or her life.

Remember the father I told you about in chapter 5, who became angry with his daughter who pushed his buttons about control? In this dad's questioning process it became clear that some of his anger came out of his fear of not having control when he was a child. As a child, he felt afraid much of the time and as he grew older he began to use his anger to control others. This gave him a false sense of control. We worked through this by asking, "Who does this belong to?" along with more questions using the clearing statement, he stopped reacting with anger to her button pushing. It is interesting to note that she also quit pushing his buttons because there weren't any buttons to push.

All the distractors of anger I am using to control, will I destroy and uncreate all of that now? Right and Wrong, Good and Bad, POD and POC, All 9, Shorts, Boys and Beyonds.®

What would life be like if we all lived in allowance of each other and stopped living in judgment of each other? Do you perceive the energy of that question? Do you feel the peace and calm it would create? Could it really be that easy? Are we willing to let it be that easy?

~11~

Just an Interesting Point of View

**"Your point of view creates your reality. Reality does
not create your point of view."**
— Gary Douglas

Gary Douglas defines consciousness as: **allowance of everything
and judgment of nothing.** Each person is entitled to their own
point of view and most of us have been raised with only two options
in life. One is to agree and align; the other is to resist and react.
How much are your kids doing one of those with your points of
view? What if there is another option? — Allowance in the way of
acknowledging a point of view as:

"It is just an interesting point of view."

Nothing more is required. It just is. When you are not in allowance, you create more chaos. Judgment is the opposite of allowance.
When kids are judged they too resist and react or align and agree,
and neither allows them to choose. Parents place judgments on their
kids that are often their own judgments of themselves. "He gets that
from me" isn't about genetics; it's about what you project onto your
child and how much of that he believes to be true. Stop and listen
to the words you say to your children. Is there a belief that the child
can pick up as a way of defining who she is? And if she agrees with
it what will she need to do to be that? If she resists it what will she
need to do to prove she isn't? Here are a couple examples:

You always make us late.

The child believes that as truth and continues to make you late.

Can you hurry up and get dressed?

The child believes that you believe she is slow and aligns to be slow. She can't help it; she now believes it to be true. When you are in allowance that it takes her longer to dress, you actually create a space from which she can choose to do something different as long as you are not imposing it. You can even use the question to offer a different possibility to show up.

What would it take for us to be dressed and out of the house in 30 minutes?

On the other hand, if the child resists buying into the belief that she is slow, she may do all she can to prove that she isn't. She may rush through everything, just to prove that she isn't slow. What if she can be slow or fast depending on what works for her? And what if none of that was a judgment, just what she chose in the moment?

When I was tutoring students I would hear parents say things to their kids as they dropped them off. One day I recall a father told his son, "Be good and do your best." As this boy took in his father's words, I saw his face drop and the light go out of his eyes. The message the father inferred was that you aren't usually good, and I have to tell you to do your best — so much judgment! This father had some interesting points of view about his son and rather than judge the father, the boy and I just acknowledged that the dad did indeed have interesting points of view. Then I asked the boy if it was true that he wasn't good or that he didn't do his best? The boy was aware enough to know what was true and when he was in allowance of his dad, he was able to do his school work with more ease.

Knowing that everything is just an **interesting point of view** is a tool we use to get out of judgment of others and of ourselves. When someone says something like, "You don't know what you're talking about!" I use the tool: **"Interesting point of view he has that point of view."** Repeating that in my head allows me to connect with the idea that, yes, it is just a point of view and doesn't require any reaction on my part. And then, if I do have a reaction or judgment that comes up, like: "Who are you to tell me that?" I say to myself, **"Interesting point of view I have that point of view."** I keep repeating that until I let go of the energy of the judgment. Teaching this tool to children is beneficial in that they now have a way of not buying into the unkind remarks that can be projected onto them from others.

Can you recall times when you could have used Interesting Point of View?

_____

_____

_____

_____

_____

_____

_____

_____

A mother told me her son came home from school and was crying because his best friend told him that he was too small to play football with him and the other boys. The mother asked me what tool she could give her child to help him through this. I shared with her two things. First, ask your child "Is that true? Are you too small to play football?" Allowing a child to uncover his own truth will empower him to see that others don't know him as well as he does. The next

95

thing I shared with her was to use, "Just an interesting point of view", and to teach her child that his friend just has a point of view, and that it is interesting and nothing more. He doesn't need to get upset by it. He doesn't have to agree with it; he can just say, **"Interesting point of view he has that interesting point of view."** Then he can choose what he would like to do next. Or ask another question: "What else is possible?" What if our children didn't buy into other people's points of view? Now whether her son gets to play with the other boys or not, he won't be judging himself or the other boy for it. He can go and create something else that will work for both of them. I am amazed over and over how kids will figure out what to do if we give them some tools.

You will find there are a number of situations where you will be able to use **Interesting Point of View,** and that it will create a different place from which to be in relationships. Play with this one whenever you listen to conversations with friends, spend time with family, and even while watching or reading the news. See what interesting points of view come up for you as well as what you notice in others. It is interesting to see what happens when we don't react or agree to the points of view of others. Sometimes they even let go of their point of view and open up to other possibilities. What else is possible?

What changes have you noticed as you continue to use these tools? Have there been changes in your relationship with your kids?

_____

_____

_____

_____

_____

_____

~12~

Ask for Help

"A little boy was having difficulty lifting a heavy stone. His father came along just then.

Noting the boy's failure, he asked, "Are you using all your strength?"

"Yes, I am," the little boy said impatiently.

"No, you are not," the father answered.

"I am right here just waiting, and you haven't asked me to help you."

As parents we are happy to help or assist our kids with their tasks, and yet many parents feel embarrassed to ask for help for themselves. At one time I felt that since my kids were "mine," I should be the one who takes care of them and never need the help of anyone else. Pretty stupid, huh? When we take that attitude, what is the message we teach our kids? Are we teaching them that we live in a community that cares for one another? Or are we teaching them that you can do it all yourself and never receive anything from anyone else? What would you like your children to learn?

What would it be like to experience true gifting and receiving by asking for help from one another with absolutely no strings attached? When I bring this up in our parent groups, people right away want to be the givers but are resistant to the idea of being the receivers. What does it mean to receive? When you ask for help or assistance, do you equate that with being less than? Do you pass judgment on yourself for not being able to take care of everything on your own?

I used to. Then I found the value of being willing to receive anything and everything without any judgment.

When my son died, I felt helpless for a long period of time. My grief had taken over to the point I couldn't even do the simplest things — shopping, laundry, phone calls, work, and meal preparation. I found myself receiving from others because I didn't have the energy to even refuse their gifts of kindness and help. I learned a lot from that experience. I learned that true giving is received with nothing attached — no obligation, just the gift of giving from another. I also began to see that I was worthy of receiving from others and that in receiving we acknowledge that we are worthy of receiving. It was through receiving that I actually became stronger, not weaker. Now as I receive more, more comes my way. Anything you are not willing to receive, will block you from receiving in other areas of your life, such as wealth, relationships, health and joy.

What am I not willing to receive that if I would receive it would give me more of what I desire in life and living? Right and Wrong, Good and Bad, POD and POC, All 9, Shorts, Boys and Beyonds.®

Just imagine for a second that you have this wonderful gift you want to offer to your best friend. You truly just want to give it to your friend and without any obligation. You care for this friend and you simply would like for her to have more because you care for her. Now imagine how you want your friend to receive it. Do you want her to receive it, just to receive it and not feel obliged in any way? Sure you do; you aren't asking for anything in return. And yet how many times do we receive from others that way? "I'll do this for you if you do this for me." And what would it be like if there was a willingness to just receive when we ask for help and guidance? Would you be willing to receive that from anyone?

- **What if by receiving from others you actually let go of any judgments you have about yourself not being capable?**

- **Would you be willing to destroy and uncreate all the areas that keep you from asking for assistance because somewhere you believe it implies that you are not capable and there must be something wrong with you if you require help?**

And everything that brings up, will you destroy and uncreate it all? Right and Wrong, Good and Bad, POD and POC, All 9, Shorts, Boys and Beyonds.®

If when you ask these questions, you get an energy that comes up, perceive it and ask the question: "Is this true for me?" If it feels light, it is true for you; if it feels heavy, it is a lie and you can now destroy and uncreate it and begin to live outside of those limitations.

How much more fun would it be to parent, if you could ask and receive support and aid when necessary? Are you willing to allow yourself the freedom to have time for yourself without your kids?

Perhaps you have heard that it takes a village to raise a child. What if you could pick your village from people that support you and your way of parenting? What if you asked for help from people who also want kids to be raised with awareness and consciousness? What questions can you ask that will bring forth the assistance and help you require?

What would it take for people who care about my kids as much as I do to show up in my life and in theirs?

Truth, do you believe you are the only one who can parent your child? Do you believe that you cannot trust anyone else with your child? Do you not trust yourself to be aware of who would make contributions to your life and your child's life? Each of these questions, along with anything else that comes up, is an opportunity to destroy and uncreate any beliefs you have held onto that keeps you from receiving, and thus making life difficult. You may also ask, "Who does this belief belong to?" And return it to sender. Some questions that may get you started are:

- **What would it take to receive more assistance raising my kids?**

- **What will it take to find a caring provider who will work for me, my children and my schedule?**

- **Who can I connect with who can help me with getting my kids to school, sports, activities, etc.?**

Asking for help models for your children that you are open to infinite possibilities in all areas and that possibilities can come from infinite sources. You can then teach your children how to choose which possibility by using the Heavy and Light tool. Teach your children to ask questions for who they would like to have help out. This empowers your children in two ways: one, they learn that you trust them to find a possibility that will work. And two, they can learn to ask for different possibilities from which they can choose.

What are some areas that you resist asking for help?

_____

_____

_____

_____

~13~

Guilt-free Parenting

"Guilt is anger directed at ourselves — at what we did or did not do."
— **Peter McWilliams**

Guilt, like worry and fear, it is a distraction from BEING YOU. It is a lie you have bought into that, for some reason, everything is your fault. When you buy into guilt, you remove the fact that people have choices and that you can't make anyone do anything they really don't want to do. How many parents lie awake at night wondering if their parenting has ruined their child?

I used to do that. I used to carry a heavy burden of guilt, believing that as a parent I **should** be able to make everything right for my kids and everyone else too. The more I carried the guilt, the more I avoided being me. I could project fault onto myself to continue to make myself wrong and pathetic. When my son died, I found it difficult to live with all the added guilt that I took from his death. I had to make a choice: die too or find another alternative. I struggled to acknowledge that it wasn't my fault and I had done my best at that time. As I began to let go of the guilt, I was able to receive the gift his death gave to me. Guilt truly distracts a person from receiving what is true.

If you live in a world of "Shoulds," you are living in guilt. How many times do you say, "I should have..." or "If only I had ... things would have turned out differently"? Can you perceive the guilt that you take on? Can you perceive how you begin to blame yourself? It doesn't discount that you have a role in your actions. But to blame yourself when things go badly doesn't help in changing the situation or allow you to let go of the judgment. When we do things that don't go well, we can stop and ask questions about how to make amends and move forward. When you live in a "Should" world, you are living in the past of what might have been. It takes you out of the present and what you have now. When I began to become aware of the effect my guilt was having on me, I would catch myself and change the word "should" to "could." For example, instead of telling myself, "I should have been nicer to that person," I change it to, "I could have said that differently. What would I like to do about this?" Can you sense the difference between the two? I hope that by now you have gotten the idea that self-judgment is a cruel punishment we dish out to ourselves. And if we would stop, life would be much different. I wonder how it would affect your children to see you be less harsh on yourself. Would it give them permission to be kinder to you and to themselves?

Now consider this: as you take on the guilt for your children's choices, you are also letting them know that they don't own any of their own actions. You actually get to train them to blame you and others for the choices that they make. I have met kids like this who have no idea that they have been the ones who have been making the choices in their life. They blame others for everything that happens to them. I wonder if you would like this for your child? The other option is to let go of your guilt and allow them to make their choices in order to gain more awareness from each choice they make. How empowering would that be?!

 There are some easy steps to remove guilt from your life. Once I began applying these steps, my life became much easier and I began to also feel much better physically. Our poor bodies take on stress in so many ways, that when we begin to let go of it other changes can happen too.

1. Acknowledge you have the guilt.

2. Ask: Is this mine or someone else's? It is rarely ever yours.

3. Clear it away: return to sender, destroy and uncreate all the places you bought it as yours.

All the distractors of guilt I have running, will I destroy and uncreate all of those now please? Right and Wrong, Good and Bad, POD and POC, All 9, Shorts, Boys and Beyonds.®

4. Choose something else: allowance, joy, peace of mind, laughter — whatever you choose to have instead of guilt.

Guilt is something a lot of people have chosen to take on. Each time you feel the sense of guilt coming on, apply the four steps and see what changes. It is a tool that will come in handy over and over. This is an area that may be beneficial writing down times and situations that you have carried guilt.

Where I do allow guilt to take over my awareness? What would I like to choose instead?

_____

_____

_____

_____

_____

_____

_____

_____

~14~

Telling the Truth

"I always tell the truth. Even when I lie."
— Al Pacino

A common complaint I hear from parents is that their child tells lies. I also had some issues with this with my own kids. I would get really upset with them because they wouldn't tell me the truth. I had a wonderful Access facilitator confront me with this question, "So what are your judgments about lying?" BAM! That hit me! All the beliefs I had about lying came rushing to the surface, and about as fast as they came, so did my justifications. "Of course it is wrong to lie; doesn't the Bible, my church, my family, my education, this society, all say it is wrong to lie?" And as I worked at trying to justify all of this, I knew deep down that the judgment was more destructive than the lie itself. I began to see that each time my son would lie to me, I went into judgment that he was wrong to lie. Ouch! Each time we make our kids wrong for something, they get to align and agree with it (which means they keep lying), or resist and react to it (which means they now have to prove something else by pulling away from you). No one gets any freer from either of those choices.

Here is a good place to introduce another tool that I have found extremely helpful.

Destroy and Uncreate Your Relationships!

I know that may sound harsh, but let me tell you more. When I went to judgment of my son for lying, I began to see me in how I handled it. I began to see that maybe judging him wasn't the best way to approach his lying. Now I had been judging him for a long time and I had delivered numerous lectures about how wrong it is to lie. Each time he lied, I judged him, and since the lying continued, that obviously wasn't working. I am sure I also instilled guilt in him for his lying. Let's just heap it all on. Once I got clear on my part and how destructive I was being, I decided to clear all the judgments I carried about that and anything else in our relationship. I began each day by saying:

"I destroy and uncreate my relationship with my son."

In doing so, I destroyed and uncreated all of the energies that weren't working for our relationship and allowed the slate to be wiped clean each day. For all the things that do work in our relationship — the gratitude, the appreciation, the cooperation, the joy, etc. — those will continue because they are contributions. When we destroy and uncreate any relationship, we only destroy and uncreate the things that aren't working, like the judgments, the fears, the anger and so on. We can't destroy the things that contribute to a relationship.

Then after destroying and uncreating, I ask:

"What contribution can I be in his life today?"

"What contribution can I receive from him today?"

The magic I have seen from this exercise in all of my relationships is worth noting. Without any added effort from me, people in my life began to also be a contribution to my life. Our connections grew deeper, and joy emerged like a blooming flower. Suddenly my son opened up and felt more comfortable talking with me, my spouse began to help me in ways I hadn't even asked for directly, and clients began showing up.

There are and there will be those days when you do or say something as a thoughtless reaction to your kids, your spouse, your friends, and others. By destroying and uncreating your relationships each day, you have the possibility to create something new and abundant in those relationships. I also apply this to my relationship with myself, and my business.

Now back to the lying. So what is your response when your child lies to you, or anyone for that matter?

 What is most important is for you to know what is true. That is why you are asking the question. If you have been using the tools, you have been getting better at being in your own knowing. So simply say **"truth"** (in your head) before you ask a child a question, and they will tell you the truth or you will know they are lying. You may never need to call them on the lie; this may be just for you so that you know what is true. Check in and see what feels light — calling them on the lie or letting it be? Follow the lightness. Refrain from making them wrong for lying; but if you are required to call them on a lie, ask them how well telling a lie worked for them?

As I used this with my son, it didn't mean that he stopped lying right away. It meant that once I stopped judging him and reacting to his lying, he felt safer telling me the truth. I also knew that while he continued to choose to lie that I could trust that he would lie to me again. We will talk more about trust soon. When I stopped expecting him to tell the truth, and I had no judgment about it, he really didn't

111

have much of a reason to lie. He sensed that I knew what was true anyway. I know this may sound way off the charts. I had tried a lot of other ideas and nothing worked until I was willing to look at myself and see what I could change about my reaction. The results speak for themselves. Letting go of our judgments creates massive change in our relationships. I wonder what it will create for you and your family. How much will it allow you to be more of you?

What does this bring up for you about telling the truth and lying?

_____

_____

_____

_____

_____

_____

_____

_____

_____

_____

_____

_____

_____

_____

_____

_____

_____

_____

_____

~15~

Discipline

**Original meaning of discipline —
to instruct.**

The original meaning of discipline is to instruct. Do you have a different sense of how these tools may create a different reality for you and your kids? By applying these tools to your life, you instruct your kids to know what is possible for them. Will it be necessary to impose punitive discipline? That is up to you. When children are punished the message they receive is that they are wrong. The lesson they have learned is that you are in control over them. They haven't had a voice about the reason they did what they did, and they haven't been empowered to look at their action as a choice that can be done differently without any judgment. If you are going to punish a child, I encourage you to ask questions about where you are coming from in that action.

- **Are you wanting to control the child because you are feeling controlled by them?**

- **Are you experiencing fear that if they don't choose something different they will have a hard life; and it is up to you to change them?**

- **Are you doing it because it is a belief you have about how to raise children?**

- ## Are you being you in this situation?

Asking questions may give you an opportunity to look at what is really coming up for you and allow you to change it, if you choose. You may also consider what it is doing to your child as well.

I am reminded by the words some parents would use when punishing a child, "This is going to hurt me a lot more than it is going to hurt you." It is interesting that we would choose to hurt ourselves when our children do something displeasing to us. I can't see the sense in that. I wonder how much confusion it creates for the child.

Parents come to me because their child has a behavior issue and they have tried everything they can think of to change it. Kids don't do things just to do them or because they are bad or want to hurt others. They do things because of how they feel and what they perceive is happening around them. Behavior is a way of communicating. If you want to change a child's behavior, you have to know what is behind it. What is the reason they are hitting other kids? What is it that they are trying to say but no one will listen?

I worked with the mother whose 4 year old was having "melt downs" at school when she didn't get her way. The school kept punishing the child for the child's actions rather than exploring and asking questions about what else could be going on. When the mother brought this to the attention of the school, they found out the girl's sugar level was dropping. They discovered that if they allowed her to have a snack more often, she didn't have the meltdowns. Just imagine the future of this girl if this had not been discovered. She certainly didn't know what was happening, but her behavior was an indicator that something needed to be addressed.

You now have a generous knapsack full of tools you can use that will not only empower your child but also give you confidence that you are empowered too. Will it take some practice? Most likely; new habits can come slowly for some of us, but the more you destroy and uncreate the patterns you have running your life, the easier it will become. We can always let our kids know that we goofed and that we would like to choose to do something differently. Be kind to yourself as you practice the tools. You wouldn't expect your child to master the piano, dance, or anything else without some spending time with it.

What are your thoughts about discipline?

_____

_____

_____

_____

_____

_____

_____

_____

_____

_____

_____

_____

_____

_____

_____

_____

_____

_____

_____

_____

_____

~16~

Five Keys to Thriving Relationships

"True intimacy has five elements:
Honor, Trust, Vulnerability, Allowance
and Gratitude."
— Dr. Dain Heer

There are five keys to creating relationships that are meaningful, happy and a true contribution to your life. This goes for any relationship, and first and foremost your relationship with yourself. If you aren't receiving these five keys for yourself, you will not be able to have them with or for anyone else. It all starts with your relationship with you. "Love others as you love yourself" is a quote from the Bible that most of us are aware of. Let's put emphasis on the words: "As you love yourself," yet how many of us have put ourselves last, somehow believing that it is more important to love others first? I know I lived many years of my life this way, and once I chose to direct nurturing attention toward myself, my relationships greatly improved. How many of you have grown up believing that if you give attention, love, caring and kindness to yourself, you are being selfish, wrong and bad? Would you like to destroy and uncreate all of that now? And while you are at it, return to sender all of it that doesn't belong to you too.

So what are the five elements needed to have an intimate, meaningful relationship, with you or anyone else? We have already talked about one of the keys — Allowance. Check in to see how much allowance you have for yourself. What if you stopped judging everything you did? How would your body feel if you were in allowance of it completely? What other areas in your life are you still judging yourself?

_____

_____

_____

_____

_____

_____

_____

_____

_____

The next one is **Gratitude**. When you are grateful, you are not in judgment, you appreciate yourself and others. Being in gratitude for all things is a life changer. When I began looking at everything — "good or bad" — with gratitude, I knew it could no longer have a hold on me. I could begin to change it and allow myself to receive from it. Having gratitude for your children at all times will open you up to receive the gift they are to your life.

If you aren't used to being in gratitude you might consider having a gratitude journal in which you begin and end each day listing 5–10 things you are grateful for. It can transform your life to start and end your day with gratitude for everything. How does it get any better than this?

Let's practice now. Think of 5 to 10 things that you are grateful for in this moment. What if you included some things about yourself too?

_____

_____

How does that feel? Do you sense that things are lighter as you turn to gratitude? Keep playing with it.

Honor is the next key. When you honor yourself you choose according to what will be to your benefit. You honor and express to others what doesn't work for you and what you won't put up with. You make choices that contribute to living a life of joy and meaning for you and others. Honor means you don't settle for less, but you do ask questions to get what you require. You don't have to validate your worth. Just by being, you are worthy. The same is true for others; you don't need them to prove anything to be honored. Their value is in their being.

The next key is **Trust**. I used to think trust meant that I could trust someone to do what I thought they should do and because I asked them to. That didn't usually work out so well. I also found that I didn't trust myself, because I kept looking to others to create my life. Now I am learning to trust myself to do what works for me regardless of the expectation of someone else. I also trust the people in my life to do what works for them. It is like trusting a frog to jump and swim and be a frog. I can't trust him to fly like a bird; that wouldn't work for the frog, even though it might be what would work for me.

In my previous marriage I had expectations that my spouse (like the frog) would change to be more of who I thought he should be. I thought I could trust him to make those changes. Looking back, I don't know where I got that idea, but I am pretty sure it had something to do with me being right and him being wrong. There was so much judgment from me and very little allowance. Because he wouldn't change, I blamed him for our marriage not working out. And yes I have destroyed and uncreated all of that. I mention it here because I created a belief about trust that was founded in judgment, not allowance. I wonder if you know of relationships who try to change others because they think it will work out better for them. You know what the funny thing is? I didn't trust myself. I am grateful to have these tools to change, choose and become more aware.

Expecting a child or spouse or partner to do something they can't or don't value is not trusting them. Trust doesn't involve judgment. It simply means knowing that people will do what will work for them, for as long as they choose it. I have found that when I let go of my judgments of others, especially around trust, that they seem to want to do things differently as a way of honoring me; even though I don't desire or require it. Less force more choice!

The final key here is **Vulnerability**. So many people resist being vulnerable as if it means they will be nailed to the cross or walked all over. To be vulnerable means that you have no barriers to anything and thereby allows you to be aware of everything. Therefore it gives you more space from which to choose. Choosing to be vulnerable allows one to be in their power and potency of being. How much easier will it be for your child to relate to you if you don't have any barriers separating the two of you?

There you have the five keys — Gratitude, Allowance, Trust, Honor and Vulnerability. Applying these keys to your life will change how you relate to yourself and others. Discover your own way of expressing gratitude and being in allowance. Discover what trust means to you and how to honor yourself and others. Explore what is missing for you in the area of vulnerability. Ask yourself questions about the areas you struggle moving into. Is there some fear that holds you back? You have a section on fear you can turn to for assistance. Do you have self-worth issues that don't allow you to honor yourself? Being in question when these keys are not coming easily to you will give you possibilities from which you will know what is true for you. Remember, what feels light is true and what feels heavy is a lie. Take a moment to write your thoughts or responses to any of the above questions.

_____

_____

_____

_____

_____

_____

_____

_____

_____

_____

_____

_____

_____

_____

_____

_____

_____

_____

~17~

Summary of

Empowered Parents Empowering Kids

A Guide to BE YOU Parenting

There you have it. Tools for BE YOU parenting. Your knapsack is now overflowing with tools. The adventure of using these tools can change all areas of your life, not just being a parent. You now have the gift of being you at all times. You get to be the YOU you choose to be. Let me be the first to offer you my appreciation for stepping into being you. You are creating more change on this planet than you will ever know. Even if we never meet you face to face; although I hope we might, I am grateful to you for the change you contribute to my life. We are all connected in this world; when one thing changes, it affects all of us in magical ways we may never know. That is how the Universe works. Let go of limitations, and choose what you would really like to have. As you practice these techniques, your confidence will grow, as will your awareness and consciousness. I also thank you for empowering your child to be the unique, awesome being he or she is here to be. It is the adventure of a lifetime, and you have a family with which to travel with you. I wish you all the best in your journey.

~ Mary Dravis-Parrish

Some reminders:

- Have allowance for yourself as a parent and for your children.

- Everything is just an interesting point of view.

- Remove guilt, fear and worry from your life.

- Say "Truth" when asking a question.

- Uncreate and destroy all your judgments of you as a parent and all judgments of your children.

- Acknowledge you and your children's gifts, talents and abilities.

- Acknowledge your children's awareness; let them know that they know.

- Fear is not real. Ask a question. Worry is always a distraction from knowing.

- Ask your children what they would like to do, what activities would their body enjoy?

- Be willing to be a "bad" parent. Are you willing to be judged?

- Use Heavy and Light when asking questions and making choices.

- Be in the question, not the answer.

- Have fun!

- Trust you to know more than you think you know.

- Have gratitude for all things — How does it get any better than this?®

Questions to change anything:

- Who does this belong to? ® Is this mine?

- If I choose this, what will my life be like in 5 years, 10 years?

- This is not working for me, what other choice is possible?

- What would it take to change this?

- How does it get any better than this?®

- What am I refusing to know about this?

- What would it take to change your grades, your ability to play sports and to be happy?

- What contribution can your kids be to the family?

- What contribution can you be to the family?

- What is right about this that I am not getting?

- What is this? What do I do about this? Can I change this? If so how?

- Is this the change I have been looking for?

"Today was good. Today was fun.

Tomorrow is another one."

~ Dr. Seuss

Other Access Consciousness® Books

Conscious Parents Conscious Kids
By Gary M. Douglas and Dr. Dain Heer

This book is a collection of narratives from children immersed in living with conscious awareness. Wouldn't it be great if you could create the space that would allow your kids to unleash their potential and burst through the limitations that hold them back? To create the ease, joy and glory in everything they do and to consciously take charge of their own lives?

The Keys to the Magic
By Anne Maxwell

If you could learn new tools to use to integrate parents into the play therapy process in a way that could facilitate healing, would you use them? What if you can be you in the play therapy room, no matter what the situation or circumstances…at ease, confident, caring, aware, totally present…regardless of who's in the room with you? As play therapists, may of us have an easier time with kids than we do with parents. *The Keys to the Magic* presents you with other possibilities.

Would You Teach a Fish to Climb a Tree?
By Anne Maxwell, Gary M. Douglas, and Dr. Dain Heer
A Different Take on Kids with ADD, ADHD, OCD and Autism. People tend to function from the point of view that there is something wrong with these children because they don't learn the way the rest of us do. The reality is that they pick things up in a totally different manner. This book takes a look at that and so much more!

Being You, Changing the World
By Dr. Dain Heer
Have you always known that something COMPLETELY DIFFERENT is possible? What if you had a handbook for infinite possibilities and dynamic change to guide you? With tools and processes that actually worked and invited you to a completely different way of being? For you? And the world?

Scan for more information

For more Access Consciousness® Books go to www.accessconsciousnesspublishing.com

About the Author

Mary Dravis-Parrish has over 25 years of experience as an educator, trainer, coach, speaker, and Access Consciousness® facilitator. Being a child, living in a home of eight children, she discovered many styles to living, learning and coping, which lead her on a path to teaching children and working with parents to create more ease in family living. Mary's parenting experiences include being a teen parent, single parent, co-parent and stepparent; she is also a parent who lost her son to suicide. She understands the needs, demands, and dynamics parents' experience. Mary has taught special education children for over 18 years and now coaches parents to utilize strategies that empower their current parenting skills, which in turn empower children and create a greater world for all of us.

Mary shares simple strategies that are highly effective, such as questioning strategies, release of expectation techniques, empowerment techniques and many more. As a certified facilitator in Access Consciousness®, family dynamics, tutoring and personal development, Mary has equipped hundreds of parents and children with her simple strategies that have empowered families to thrive, have less chaos and more confidence. Applying her BE YOU parenting strategies, trainings and the tools of Access Consciousness®, she facilitates change in people's lives, so they have more confidence, awareness, joy and fun in all areas of living.

For more information contact:

Mary Dravis-Parrish

Certified Facilitator of Access Consciousness®

Parent Whisperer

Simple Strategies for Family Living

EnhancedLivingNow.com

parentwhispers@gmail.com

Mary is available for classes, sessions and speaking.